Point of Attack

Point of Attack
The Defense Strikes Back

Harry Carson
and Jim Smith

McGraw-Hill Book Company
New York   St. Louis   San Francisco
Hamburg   Mexico   Toronto

1 2 3 4 5 6 7 8 9 D O C D O C 8 7 6

ISBN 0-07-010227-9

LIBRARY OF CONGRESS CATALOGING-IN-PUBLICATION DATA

Carson, Harry.
  Point of attack.
  1. New York Giants (Football team)   I. Smith, Jim.
II. Title.
GV956.N4C37   1987   796.332′64′097471   86-20829
ISBN 0-07-010227-9

Contents

Acknowledgments

WITHOUT HARRY CARSON, the most unfathomable athlete I've ever met, I still would be dreaming about my first book. Without his sensitivity, perception and physical skill, it would not have been worth the trouble.

I would like to recognize all who helped shape the writer I am: primarily my parents, Arthur and Dorothy; Jim Swartz, the teacher who helped a class clown mature; reporters such as Bob Rubin, George Vecsey, Joe Donnelly, Tim Moriarty, Bob Waters, Joe Gergen and Dave Anderson, whose work I respect; Giants' beat reporters Vinnie DiTrani, Hank Gola, Greg Garber and Barry Stanton, with whom I was locked in friendly combat for six seasons; my successor at *Newsday*, Peter King, and the *Newsday* editors who have cut me down to size—especially Sandy Padwe and Dick Sandler.

I would like to say a special thank-you to transcriber Virginia Chepak; to my agent Mel Berger of the William Morris Agency; to my friend David Fishof; and to senior editor Tom Quinn and the rest of the staff at McGraw-Hill.

J. R. S.

Point of Attack

1 Introduction

GIANTS FANS tell me I'm a throwback player. I'm flattered that they compare me to Hall of Famers like Ray Nitschke, Dick Butkus, and Sam Huff. I'm old-fashioned in a lot of ways. I don't smoke, drink, or use drugs. I'm religious. People tell me I'm sensitive and caring. But on a football field, I undergo a metamorphosis. My job is knocking people down. I'm a linebacker in the National Football League. And I'm good at my job.

I guess I look a little scary with my helmet on. I never smile on the field. My opponents look across the line, see my white facemask and all this darkness behind it—except for my two little brown eyes. A reporter once wrote that my stare is so penetrating that my eyes "seem capable of entering your mind and rattling your brain into submission."

I never talk to opponents or help them up after a play. Why spend energy helping a guy up when you work so hard to put him down? That adds to my eerie image. On a football field, I am absolutely fearless. I love the playing part, the game. When my name is announced and the fans are cheering, that time is mine; I'm the center of attention. When I've got somebody by the throat (not literally, of course) and I'm squeezing, it's a very good feeling.

But my name isn't Hacksaw, Dr. Doom, Dirt, or Monster. Just plain Harry. I still have all my teeth. I rarely do anything spectacular. I hardly ever blitz the quarterback. I stop the run. I wrap running backs up and lay them down. Like Huff, Nitschke, and Butkus did. I am a mainstay on the Giants' goal-line defense, where only the toughest perform. I am not afraid to put my helmet into a guy's chest. In football parlance, I can deliver the blow.

A 1981 study of football players and nonathletes at a college in the Southwest Conference found that linebackers are more hostile and aggressive than players at other positions and that they scored significantly higher than all others tested in depression, anger, fatigue, and confusion. I don't think I fit the mold. I'm even-tempered. A reporter once described me as "a social worker trapped inside a football player's body."

Some guys meet me off the field and can't believe I'm not Darth Vader's brother. I don't breathe fire. I have about four personalities. I have two on the field. One is quite vocal; another is very quiet. It depends on the situation. I used to be very nervous and uptight before games. Now I'm cool and relaxed. I do my best to transmit that feeling to my teammates and help them get the most from themselves.

One of the biggest problems I have is turning the hostility on and off. I always go to church on game mornings. I sit there, listening to the organist and the sermon, and I get tranquil. Deep inside myself. Then I have to drive to Giants Stadium, forget that mood, and get tough. I have to concentrate on punishing my opponent. One of my former teammates use to call me "H.C.," for "hot and cold." But you can't walk around feeling hostile all the time. At least I can't.

I've never been the kind to taunt an opponent. I think that would just be wasted energy. And I've never been taunted by anybody. I've survived ten years in pro football and have the scars and pains to prove it. But I've retained my sense of humor and perspective. I've become a team leader because of what I do on the field. That has allowed me to be more vocal the past couple of years in the dressing room and the huddle.

The Giants have had three winning seasons in my career, all in the last five years. I know what it's like to suffer. There have been many times when I felt like walking away. In 1980 I almost did. There have been many times when I just had to free my mind of football, by listening to music or reading the paper—not just the sports section—to get my mind off the game. Because it can be all-consuming. Now I think this season the Giants can make a run at the Super Bowl. All of the elements finally are in place. I felt we were on the brink of being a championship team in 1985, when I began this diary. I thought I might be able to dispel a few mistaken notions about life in the NFL. I don't have any startling revelations about drugs, sex, booze, or pills. Just a typical season seen through my eyes.

I've been a loner for most of my career. Most of my teammates do not know any more about me than they see in the dressing room or on the field. I don't reveal much of myself to them—by choice. The NFL is so transient that it's hard to get close to anybody. The disappointment of losing them in trades or cuts hurts too much, so I've kept my distance.

If this book has a topic sentence, it is this: Under the helmets, the pads, and the sweaty T-shirts, most football players are caring people who are sensitive to their own needs and to the needs of others. They aren't all raving maniacs, psychopaths, drug addicts, alcoholics, or gamblers. Unfortunately, the guys with problems usually are the ones who get the publicity.

Success rarely comes overnight in the NFL. The process of reaching the Super Bowl usually takes several years. The seeds are planted via the college draft. A good group of players matures together. Their record improves gradually. The team experiences the disappointment of falling just short—and at last, it arrives. Look at the Chicago Bears. They improved from 3–6 in the strike-shortened 1982 season, to 8–8 in 1983, to 10–6 in 1984. They got bounced from the 1984 playoffs, 23–0, by the San Francisco 49ers in the National Football Conference title game. But the Bears regrouped, went 15–1 in 1985, and went on to win Super Bowl XX, beating the Giants, 21–0, en route in the NFC semifinals. "If the Bears can improve that much in one year," our co-owner Wellington Mara said after the 1985 season, "so can we." I agree. I think we can be the Bears of 1986 and go all the way.

If any NFL owner deserves a championship, it is Mara. He is so much a part of football that the NFL once named the ball "The Duke" in his honor. His father Jack founded our franchise in 1925. Wellington's earliest memory of the team was from that year when he was nine years old. He remembers his father standing in front of church after mass and saying, "I'm going to try to put football over in New York today."

He did. The Giants have experienced plenty of ups and downs since then. I see us now as a team on the threshold of a dream. That's inspiring. I think my body has only two or three more years of linebacking left in it. You know there's a time limit, but you don't know when your time's going to run out. I know I'll feel it on the field. My legs won't have the same power. I won't be able to cover backs downfield. I'll know.

For now, my experience helps tremendously. Sometimes I'll see a play develop and I'll flash back to a similar play from five or six years before. What I did then, I find myself doing again, like playing off a block and diving at the ballcarrier. I still feel good. I can cover Joe Morris 20 yards down the field in practice. I doubt I'll play as many as five more years. I won't be the Charlie Joiner of linebackers, but I'll play as long as I'm contributing and having fun.

I think all inside linebackers do the same things. Of course some are more effective than others. I think toughness is what's enabled me to survive and excel. I've avoided serious injury in my career because I've been in better shape than most of my opponents. And I protect myself on the field. Some guys have no respect for their bodies. When I'm out there, I play under control, like a veteran linebacker should. I try to stay away from piles, where I might be hit from behind in the back or the knees. I'm constantly moving, looking out for myself. Sometimes I have to accept a lick to protect myself. Like if I'm trying to get to a ballcarrier and I see that a blocker has a good shot at my knees. I have to surrender, forget about the play, protect myself. That's what I mean by playing smart.

I don't think I'm going to walk away from football with a cane, like Jim Otto of the Raiders. I hope I won't need a series of operations, like he had, to put my body back together. I'll hurt, but I think I'll be able to handle it. My knees hurt from the pounding they've taken on artificial surfaces. My shoulders ache from years of tackling. My neck hurts. When I bend over to wash my face, I have trouble straightening up. That's the price I've had to pay. But it's been worth it.

There's nothing I'd like better than to cap my career with a championship in Super Bowl XXI. I view my career as a ladder. I know I'm on the down-side, but I'm still an important contributor. So I don't worry about being cut from the team. Not yet. The Giants aren't going to trade me, because of what I represent. I am a link to their glory years. Some say I'm the embodiment of the team: EveryGiant. A lot of fans remember that I was one of the team's bright spots when not much good was happening. When the time comes, I think club officials will just tell me to retire and I'll go out with a gold watch. I want to bow out with grace. Maybe the Giants will retire my number, 53. Our trainer, John Dziegiel, fires me up before games by telling me I'm just as good as Huff and those other guys were. John's seen a lot of players come and go. He knows what it takes to get it done in the NFL, so I respect his opinion. When I take the field, I feel I have to play at an all-pro level because I'm carrying the torch.

Other voices: Beasley Reece, a teammate from 1977–1983, compared Carson to a battery, saying, "The boy is the ultimate in middle linebackers. The right height (6'3"), the exact weight (245). He's not mean and nasty as much as strong and consistent. Everybody draws strength from him.''

I've always tried to show a good example to my teammates, regardless of the score, whether we're ahead or behind. I only know how to play at one speed—full out. Naturally I hope I've done enough to be considered for the Pro Football Hall of Fame in Canton, Ohio, when I retire: seven Pro Bowls in my first ten years. But before all that, I'd like to play in a Super Bowl.

I started thinking about that in our dressing room at Chicago's Soldier Field this past January 5, amid the crush of scribbling reporters, smelly, discarded uniforms, rolled up tape, and equipment bags. Sitting on an equipment trunk, surveying the scene and answering a television reporter's questions, I flashed ahead to training camp, 1986. I couldn't wait.

The Giants had only two winning seasons between 1964 and 1980. But now we've put back-to-back winning seasons together—9–7 and 10–6—for the first time since 1962–1963. So even though the Bears shut us out in the playoffs and they're as young a team overall as we are, I'm optimistic. There were too many positives for us in 1985 not to be optimistic about this season. Our defense was No. 2 statistically in the NFL to Chicago's and never has been better. We finally developed a strong running game with 5'7", 195-pound Morris running behind our "suburban offensive line." He set club records with 1,336 rushing yards and 21 touchdowns. Our quarterback, Phil Simms, stayed healthy for the second straight year and made his first Pro Bowl, where he was named MVP.

We lost six regular-season games in 1985 by a total of 20 points. We were competitive every week. We should improve with age. If some of our rookie draftees contribute and we catch some breaks in 1986, we could go 13–3! It will be very hard for the Bears to duplicate last season—emotionally and physically. Only three teams have won back-to-back Super Bowls: Green Bay (I and II), Miami (VII and VIII), and Pittsburgh (IX and X, XIII and XIV).

There were times in my career when I never thought I'd reach this point. In my first five seasons, 1976 through 1980, we had records of 3–11, 5–9, 6–10, 6–10, and 4–12. I asked to be traded, was refused and pondered retirement in 1980. Coach Ray Perkins and psychologist Frank Ladata talked me out of it. We were 4–5 in 1982 and 3–12–1 the next year. I asked to be traded again after the 1983 season. General manager George Young told me I was too valuable to trade.

Now that we finally are a contender, I wish I was younger. I'll be 33 in November. George Martin was 33 in February. He expects to come back for the 1986 season, so I'll remain the Giants' second-oldest player in 1986. Only one starting linebacker in the league is older, the Patriots' 35-year-old Steve Nelson. Nobody has to tell me my time in football is short. My body whispers it to me every morning. I look OK but I can feel my bones clanking inside.

I know the Giants have to start grooming somebody to replace me. Maybe it will be our No. 2 1986 pick, Pepper Johnson of Ohio State, a 6'3", 247-pound run-stopper. Pro football is a business. I found that out a long time ago. But when I retire, I'd like to do it right. I hope I don't suffer a Joe Theismann-type broken leg injury and it ends suddenly. I hope I'm fortunate enough to be like Randy Gradishar and announce at the beginning of a season that it will be my last. I might do that in 1987. But I'm taking it one year at a time. I don't have a timetable. A lot depends on how long it takes for the Giants to find a replacement.

I've been a Giant long enough to know that anything can happen. One of our brightest prospects, Troy Archer, was killed in a truck accident in 1979. We've had three players' careers ended by cancer. Doug Kotar died of an inoperable brain tumor. The others, Dan Lloyd and John Tuggle, never had a chance to fulfill their promise. We had a running backs' coach, Bob Ledbetter, die after suffering a stroke a few years ago. Our team doctor, John Marshall, was killed in a plane crash.

I'm sure after he started every game for us in 1984, center Kevin Belcher expected to have a long NFL career. But he was in an auto accident before the 1985 season, suffered nerve damage in a leg, and was released early in 1986. So was Tuggle. So I take nothing for granted. I try not to live my life in the future. I savor every moment, every game, every tackle.

Two things bother me. One is that several other teams that have been down in the ashes have risen up from the grave and gone to Super Bowls in a short time. The Redskins were 6–10 in 1980; two years later, they won the Super Bowl. The 49ers went from 2–14 in 1979 to a Super Bowl victory two years later. Cincinnati went from 6–10 in 1980 to 12–4 and the Super Bowl a year later.

Another thing that bugs me is that a lot of players who weren't good enough to play for the Giants or were traded have later played in Super Bowls and I haven't. Guys like Craig Morton with the Denver Broncos, Fred Dryer with the Los Angeles Rams, Todd Christensen and Odis McKinney with the Los Angeles Raiders, Joe Pisarcik with the Philadelphia Eagles, Otis Wonsley and Alvin Garrett with the Washington Redskins, and Emery Moorehead last season with the Chicago Bears.

The Giants played in six NFL championship games between 1956 and 1963, winning one. They had an overall record of 73–25–4. When the fans tell me I'm a throwback, they also mean I'm a link with old-time Giants of that era like Huff, Dick Modzelewski, Rosey Grier, and Jim Katcavage. I hope we can reward the fans who have stuck by us all these years by starting a championship era of our own. I know that injuries, bad breaks, or a bad draft crop could send us back to square one. I hope there's a carry-over from the past two seasons, but you never know. On our flight home from Chicago, the No. 1 engine on our left wing had a flameout ten minutes before we landed at Newark Airport. Most of the guys did not know what was happening. I remember looking around and thinking that there would be some new faces in those seats in 1986. Most teams turn over ten to 15 players a year on their 45-player rosters. I knew I had played my last game with as many as a third of them. We finished the 1985 season with 20 first- and second-year players. More youth will be phased in during 1986.

When we landed, playing cards littered the floor of the plane. Most of the guys were playing poker and weren't aware that fire trucks lined the runway. "I wish they would have told us so I could have said my prayers," Gary Reasons said.

I felt empty when I got home. I still had X's and O's floating around in my mind. I don't like to look back. But I wish we had been able to sustain the emotion in Chicago that we had displayed while besting the 49ers the previous week at Giants Stadium. Now *that* game was a thrill. One of the highlights of my career.

Game No. 17

Giants 17
San Francisco 3

Running on All Cylinders

THIS VICTORY WAS the highlight of our 1985 season. All pistons were churning. I was impressed with everybody on our team. We had confidence, we were concentrating and we were hitting people. We had more intensity on defense that day than I've seen on any Giants' team I've played on. We attacked the 49ers for 60 minutes. And this was a team which had won two Super Bowls in four years and had beaten us five straight times; two of those losses bounced us from the playoffs in 1981 and 1984.

The first thing I noticed when we began our preparations for the 49ers on Wednesday, Christmas Day, was their long injury report. Their best offensive lineman, guard Randy Cross, was out after knee surgery. Rookie Tory Nixon would start at left cornerback for Pro-Bowler Eric Wright, who had injured a knee. Right cornerback Ronnie Lott would be playing with a cast over his fractured left pinky. The 49ers had been beaten up in their last regular-season game, a 31–16 victory over Dallas.

As a player, you dismiss injury reports. You prepare as if all your opponent's available players will play on Sunday. I've seen situations where teams inflate injury reports to lull you into a false sense of security. The 49ers tried it for this game.

They listed running back Wendell Tyler as "very doubtful" for our game, since he had undergone minor knee surgery two weeks prior. (He wound up being their leading ground-gainer against us, with ten carries for 61 yards!) We knew he would play and we prepared to defend against him.

The Giants have sold out every game since 1959, an unbelievable record. Giants' tickets are the toughest to come by in New York. They have been handed down from father to son. although the team had not played a home playoff game since 1962, when it was headquartered at Yankee Stadium. The Giants lost to Green Bay 16–7 that year for the NFL title. Giants' fans of that era had no inkling that their team was in for a long period of decline.

"It was freezing that day," 51-year-old investment broker Bill Doran told *Newsday*'s George Usher in the parking lot before our game against the 49ers. "It was a long time ago, but I absolutely felt I'd see another home playoff game. I've always kept the faith. I've got $4,000 worth of ticket stubs and a lot of tailgating parties for memories."

The franchise moved to Giants Stadium in the Meadowlands in East Rutherford, New Jersey, in 1976 but kept "New York" in its name. Our fans went with us. They remember the glory years of Y.A. Tittle, Charley Conerly, Frank Gifford, Alex Webster, Del Shofner, and Rosie Brown.

In 1978, a man chartered a plane to fly over the stadium to protest 15 years of lousy football. Others burned tickets in disgust. They had a right. It seemed as though everybody was against us then, but you couldn't really blame them. We weren't just losing games, we were giving them away. It was humiliating. We stunk.

But that was a long time ago.

We were a different team in 1985. We knew we could beat the 49ers. Betty Morgan knew that. She has sat in the first row of seats behind our bench at Giants Stadium since I've been with the team. Sometimes when good things happen on the field, I'll smile or wink at her and she'll smile back.

I remember in 1984, after we beat Dallas, 28–7, to become 2–0 for the first time in 16 years, I went over to the railing and looked up. "Do you know how good I feel right now?" I asked her. She said, "Yes, I can feel it, too." I got a letter from her once. She told me her husband was a long-time fan and that she had continued coming to games after he died. That's loyalty.

We and our fans knew the 49ers were not the 13–3 team they had been in 1981 nor the awesome 15–1 club of 1984. They had struggled to a 10–6 record in 1985, same as us. And our guys wanted to pay them back for a 21–10 loss they hung on us in San Francisco the previous season in the NFC semifinals at Candlestick Park. I scored our only touchdown that day on an interception return. It was small consolation.

Near the end of a season, it comes down to the survival of the fittest. Everybody is sore. It is just a matter of degree. The length of an NFL season is absurd—four preseason games, 16 in the regular season, and a possibility of four playoff games. They should give us suits of armor. Our safety, Terry Kinard, played against the 49ers with a cast over his left thumb. Many of the rest of us had bumps and bruises.

Our offense was happy to get wide receiver Lionel Manuel back after he had spent four weeks on the injured reserve list with a pulled hamstring. Lionel was our leading receiver in the regular season, with 49 catches when he went down. The injury cost him a shot at being named to the Pro Bowl.

Lionel wears a cute little earring. I'm glad it's in his ear, not mine. I'm from the old school that says football players don't do things like that. But more and more players are wearing them. Two other teammates wear them—Jerome Sally and William Roberts. They're too big for me to kid them about it.

Manuel was the 171st player chosen in the 1984 draft, selected in the seventh round, from tiny University of Pacific. The qualities that made him instantly effective were his speed, toughness, and cutting ability. "When Lionel makes a cut," Phil Simms said, "and he's coming out of it, he's coming out running. If you can hit him in stride, you're going to get big plays."

"Deep down," said Manuel, "I can't believe I'm at this level, doing this well." He started six of our last 10 games as a rookie in 1984, catching 33 passes for 619 yards. He had 31 catches for an NFL-high 590 yards at the halfway mark of the 1985 season. By being such a deep and intermediate receiving threat, he loosened defenses and opened up room for our running attack.

I never thought Manuel and another rookie receiver, Bobby Johnson, would emerge as quickly as they did in 1984. Bobby was signed as a free agent out of Kansas. Both are gutsy. They concentrate. They're not afraid to go across the middle. They can take a hit and hang onto the ball, and they keep getting up after taking hard licks. Neither has blazing speed, but they really made defenses respect our passing attack. This gave Joe Morris more room to run.

Our guys had a laugh two days before the game when 49er quarterback Joe Montana said—via the *New York Post*—that Simms is too cocky for his own good. "Every time we play them," Montana was quoted, "our defense does a fairly good job, and every time, he says the same thing: 'We could have beaten you. If we had a little more time, I could have thrown the ball up and down the field any time I wanted to.' I mean, for a guy our defense has played well against, he's got confidence bordering on cockiness.''

Montana is right, but that's what we like about Phil—his cockiness. Cockiness only takes you so far, though. Phil also has proved himself on the field the past two seasons, throwing for about 8,000 yards. I've always felt that Simms has the tools to take us to a Super Bowl. He showed great courage and dedication by coming back from injuries which limited him to only 34 starts from 1979 through 1983. We had only one winning season in that time.

You can always tell it's Monday by the bruises on Simms' body. I feel sorry for him when I walk into the locker room and see black and blue marks all over him. He definitely earns his pay. Simms is the kind of guy who improves every time he practices. He has a strong arm, good touch and he's gotten better at reading defenses. He gets us fired up when we see him excited. He'll be 31 in 1986 and should be entering his prime.

Phil hardly fits the Joe Namath image that some New York quarterbacks have tried to live up to in the past 15 years. Simms enjoys spending time with his wife and two children at their four-bedroom colonial home in Franklin Lakes, N.J. One time he refused to have his photo taken at a charity function in a Manhattan nightclub because he did not want young fans to get the wrong impression of him. Phil likes to have fun, but he's a big family man, a solid character.

"I have no ambitions of being an off-the-field star," Simms said. "I don't want to go out and seek publicity for anything other than playing. I don't want to become any personality. It's just not in me.

"I think Joe Namath ruined it for all of us," Simms said. "That's the image everybody thinks New York quarterbacks should have: the playboy. I guess it got to be a stereotype. But he was that. I am not that. What I am is not something that makes headlines . . . Namath was leading the life that everybody deep down wishes they could. But it's not me."

The years Phil was hurt I got used to being home in Florence, S.C. for Christmas. Not the past two years. After our 1984 season we celebrated Christmas at a hotel in Fresno, where we practiced between playoff games in Anaheim and San Francisco.

The reporters who stayed with us celebrated Christmas at a Chinese restaurant. The club later bought them sweaters with their name and a "Fresno Five" logo on each one, commemorating their time in captivity. Christmas in Fresno was no picnic for us players, either.

Preparing for a playoff game during Christmas week is not really a distraction. We just make the holiday secondary. Our head coach, Bill Parcells, told reporters, "I don't give a damn about Christmas. I didn't care about Christmas shopping or any of that other crap. I told the players that.'"

Parcells, 45 years old, is where he wants to be. He was born in Englewood, New Jersey and was a three-sport athlete at River Dell High in Oradell. He grew up rooting for the Giants. He played college football at Wichita State in landlocked Kansas, coached in the heart of Texas, at West Point and at the Air Force Academy. But he favors nautical imagery. His favorite phrase is "an even keel." That's his approach with us. He doesn't get too high when we win or too low when we lose. He wants us to be that way, too. When we lose, he finds something good in the films. When we win, he corrects mistakes. An even keel. He explained the source of his analogies.

"I collect nautical objects," Parcells said. "Pictures of ships, bells, wheels, pictures of lighthouses. I don't know why. I just like them . . . I rant and rave after we win. I tell them, 'Don't believe what the newspapers say about how good you are.' Then, when the reporters are telling them they're bad, I'm telling them the opposite. I think it's my job to keep it in the proper perspective."

"In every respect," George Martin said of Parcells, "he has an even temperament. But on game day, it's the Jekyll–Hyde syndrome. He's very emotional, very vocal, very nervous. He reacts to everything. He's made it clear he's the authority out there. But no matter how vocal he becomes, after the game, it's all over. You know that if he's chewed you out, he'll probably come up and pat you on the butt the next day."

I think Bill's strength is his ability to communicate, to get along with and understand players. He makes you feel relaxed. He was a player himself, so he can identify with our problems. And yet he can be tough when he has to be. I know he has threatened to release several fringe players if they did not perform better. One was Elvis Patterson. Elvis responded positively. Some players play better when they're under a microscope. Some don't. Parcells usually pushes the right button.

He has a good but suspicious relationship with our general manager, George Young. Young let Parcells dangle after we went 3–12–1 in the injury-riddled 1983 season, not giving the coach a public vote of confidence. Young said he did not feel it was necessary. Why? Parcells thought Young was trying to deflect the media's heat from the general manager to the coach.

"Think about it," Parcells said.

"All that's nonsense," Young said.

Parcells is a businessman. Sources said that before the 1985 season
the Giants extended his contract through 1988 with annual salaries reported at $250,000, $275,000, $300,000, and $325,000. According to
a survey of 14 NFL head coaches, their average pay for 1985 was
$432,000, led by San Francisco's Bill Walsh ($900,000) and Miami's
Don Shula ($800,000). So Bill has a long way to go.

In 1985 he drove us to the franchise's highest victory total in 22
years. We had closed out our regular season with a victory over the
Steelers on a Saturday. I remember in the old days, when the Steelers
were winning four Super Bowls in a six-year stretch (1974–1979), I
couldn't even walk after playing them. I usually went right to bed. But
after this year's game, I went out shopping. I bought some wood, came
home, made a fire, did my laundry, and cooked some supper. I was so
fresh and relaxed, it was as if I had only gone for a jog, not played a
game. I guess the Steelers aren't as tough as they used to be.

On Sunday morning, a limousine picked me up and drove me to
Manhattan to appear as a guest host on the "NFL Today" show on
CBS television. It was a great experience. I think I made a good impression. It's part of trying to build a national image—which isn't easy if
you're not white, a quarterback, or colorful like the Jets' Mark Gasti-
neau. I was not paid for my television work, but I figured they were
doing me a favor.

Going into the studio and knowing that 90 million people were
watching me was a scary experience. If I made a mistake, I couldn't
take it back. I had to convince myself to relax. I think I succeeded.
Brent Musburger and Jimmy (the Greek) Snyder put me at ease. I just
played off their comments.

There were 10 monitors with no sounds, and we were watching a
number of games at once. We did several shows for different markets.
At the end, Musburger told me I did a good job. He asked me if I'd
ever considered going into broadcasting. I said I might, but I don't really
think I will.

I had an endorsement deal with Nike. It expired after the 1984
season. I once had myself up on a Nike billboard in Times Square.
How many guys can say that? A pro basketball player like Michael
Jordan, Julius Erving, Larry Bird or Patrick Ewing can make millions
with a shoe-endorsement deal. Football players make pittances by com-
parison. I guess it's because there are so many of us. I was only earning
$5,000 a year from Nike, plus a percentage of the profits on the shoes
I wore. That percentage gave me between $800 and $3,000 extra per
season.

Some other companies have approached me about wearing their

shoes. But I've gotten used to Nikes, so I think I'll keep wearing them. Now I'm free to "spat," which is taping my ankles, covering the logo of the shoes. Some players actually wear Adidas, paint over the stripes, spat, and put on another company's logo over the tape. Then they accept endorsement money from that company. The company doesn't care— as long as the right logo is on display. There's little a shoe company can do, anyway. A Philadelphia Eagle wore a different brand of shoe on each foot in Super Bowl XV and got two checks. What were they going to do, sue him? It wasn't worth the negative publicity.

We had Monday off but I decided to go to the stadium and lift weights, anyway. I needed the workout to loosen up my body and relax my muscles. There were about 12 or 15 guys in there. Some were injured and decided to lift while they were in for treatment. Others lifted because they had nothing better to do. Lifting releases tension.

Years ago there were no off-season conditioning programs. Players started getting ready for training camp in June. Hardly anybody did much weight lifting. Now it's almost mandatory. Guys start getting ready for the season in March. They lift in the off-season to acquire strength. They lift during the season to maintain it.

I don't live in the city. None of our players do. It would be tough commuting to East Rutherford to practice. I prefer the comfort and quiet of the suburbs in Ossining, N.Y., and Westwood, N.J., where I maintain homes. I like my neighbors. I don't worry about break-ins. I'd rather live like I do than in some high-rise. I can afford to live in the city. I just wouldn't be comfortable there. I also prefer jeans and sweatsuits to three-piece suits and McDonald's to the Four Seasons. I don't feel I have to impress anybody.

Each player earned $6,000 for playing in the first-round playoff game and $10,000 more for the next round. But money really isn't the incentive at times like this. Pride is. The $6,000 was not a primary thought of mine. I'd already put it in my budget. I counted on us making the playoffs.

The playoff bonus represented only two per cent of my $300,000 annual salary and was roughly one-third of what I received per game. But there were a lot of guys with five-digit salaries to whom it meant much more. Reserve linebacker Andy Headen and starting left corner-back Elvis Patterson were each making $75,000, so $16,000 for two games seemed like a nice Christmas present to them.

There are a lot of salary inequities on the Giants. I will discuss them in greater detail later. But I'll say right now that I was very upset because I was the tenth-highest-paid player on the team in 1985. Simms made the most, $900,000. Linebacker Lawrence Taylor earned $750,000. Rookie running back George Adams earned $725,000, including a signing bonus. Bart Oates, a center, earned $350,000, including bonuses. This whole situation gave me many sleepless nights, but I put it aside during the playoffs.

I spent several nights during the week watching film of 49ers' running back Roger Craig, who had become the first player in the NFL's 61-year history to surpass 1,000 yards in both rushing and receiving in the same season. When a reporter asked me what my plan was for stopping Craig, some lyrics from a "Police" song came to mind:

> *Every breath you take,*
> *Every move you make,*
> *Every bond you break,*
> *Every step you take,*
> *I'll be watching you.*

The idea with Craig was to contain him, not let him make a big play. When Montana is under a heavy pass rush, he likes to dump the ball off in the flats to Craig, who has a knack of making people miss open-field tackles. We wanted to anticipate the dump-offs, come up quickly, and stop Craig before he could get up a head of steam.

I watched film of two 49er games in 1984 and four films of 1985 games. We ran a couple of coverages in practice in which I shadowed "Craig" wherever he went. Different guys simulated 49ers' plays in practice on our scout team. Adams, Lee Rouson, Joe Morris, and Tony Galbreath all took turns being Craig. A team's reserves usually are enlisted for the scout team.

Since the NFL contracted its roster size from 49 to 45 players before the 1985 season as a cost-cutting measure, I often found myself enlisted for the scout team when it came time to simulate opponents' defenses. You've got enough to worry about without having to do that. After practices in 1985 I found myself being drained mentally and physically more than ever. There was talk of increasing the roster size, but the NFL rejected the idea in August 1986.

The thing I remembered about Craig was that in our Monday Night game in 1984 on national television, when the 49ers beat us 31–10, Craig caught a flare-out pass against me to his right. I had a bad angle, he cut inside and took it in for a score. I did not want that to happen again. It was embarrassing. I gained some revenge in the playoffs that year when I intercepted the pass and scored our only touchdown. En route to the end zone, I faked out Craig.

I wanted to have another big game. So did the rest of our defense. We practiced a new defensive formation for the 49ers called "Clemson," because that's where Headen went to college and he would be a big part of the new alignment.

We expected the 49ers to pass a lot on first down. Our usual starters at left defensive end and left inside linebacker, Curtis McGriff and Gary Reasons, are excellent defenders against the run. But we planned to use George Martin and Headen more in this game because they are better pass-rushers. It's nice to have depth. You can't win without it.

Saturday night at the hotel, I asked coach Parcells if I could talk to the team. Every week we chart our defensive goals for the next game. This time, I invited the offense to set goals with us. The offensive goals were to get 150 yards rushing, 250 passing, and not to allow any sacks.

I told the players that every team in our division had had a chance at glory. The Eagles went to the Super Bowl in 1980. The Redskins went after the 1982 and 1983 seasons. The Cowboys have had 20-straight winning seasons and has been to five Super Bowls. I just felt like it was our turn.

I told them we could not dwell on what had happened in previous games against the 49ers because we were a better team now and we had to go out and kick their asses, just knock the shit out of them.

I think I got to some of the guys, because they were very intense, very attentive. It was like a pep talk. I used quite a few four-letter words. Martin told me I said some things he really wanted to say but was too shy. I pointed to several guys and got personal.

I told Simms a lot of people were saying he can't win the big games, this is a big game, and he was going to win it. I told him I had confidence in his receivers, his line, and his backs, especially Joe Morris. I said, "Hey, you guys know we should be 15–1 or 14–2. Everybody's underestimating the Giants." I urged them all to concentrate, have confidence in each other and play to the best of their abilities, play the most physical game of their careers.

I've been doing this the past few years. A lot of players want to say things but don't have it within them to do it. So I took on the role. Casey Merrill and Carl Banks aren't afraid to speak their minds, either. They had caps made up for the whole team for this game. There was a picture of a football on each cap with the words "New York Giants" and "Playoffs." Under the football was the phrase "Strictly Business."

We did not know how badly beaten up Montana was until we read the papers after the game. He took a series of cortisone shots Friday and Saturday and a bunch of pain-killing injections in his ribs before the kickoff. His right shoulder and his left rib cage were heavily taped. Every time he coughed during the week, he was in pain. But he went all the way against us.

Our mood approaching the game and in the pregame warmups was light and confident. We had a good week of practice. Our game plan was to have our defensive ends take wide rushes to prevent Montana from scrambling outside them. And to smother Craig. We were loose. We felt no pressure because we were underdogs. Somebody wrote on the blackboard in our dressing room:

$10,000
I NEED THE MONEY.

I'm not sure whether Len Fontes wrote it, but the phrase "I need the money" became associated with him. Len is our popular defensive back coach. He was always saying that he needed the $10,000 because he was renovating his home, his wife likes to shop, and his kid wants to go to college.

We went out and earned that money. One of our defensive goals always is to shut down the opponent—three downs and out—on its first series. And we did that.

Montana threw an incompletion on first down. I stopped Craig after a four-yard gain on a second-down pitch to the right. And cornerback Ted Watts stopped Jerry Rice one yard short of a first down on a third-down pass to the right. Watts was in the game because Patterson had turned an ankle covering the opening kickoff. He fell awkwardly over 49er Keith Fahnhorst's legs on our artificial surface.

The first time we had the ball, Simms took the offense from his 36 to the 49ers' 30, and we got a 47-yard field goal from Eric Schubert. It was 3–0. I couldn't remember the last time we had a lead against the 49ers.

In their next next series, Montana completed a 20-yard pass to Dwight Clark, two short passes to tight end Russ Francis and Craig gained eight yards on a run off right tackle. They had a second-and-one at our 38. But we made two big plays in a row.

On second down, Leonard Marshall dropped Craig for a one-yard loss on a draw play. I had called a stunt on the play and Marshall shifted right into Craig's path. On third-and-two, Byron Hunt and I stopped Craig for no gain on a pitch to the right. San Francisco had to punt. We felt we were winning the battle at the point of attack.

My job is to read the play, decide which hole they're trying to attack, and plug it. That's the point of attack. That's the moment I live for.

The hit I made on Craig was like having an orgasm. I remember adjusting because one back went in motion. They were trying to overload the strong side and get more blockers out there in front of me. I started running laterally just before the ball was snapped, anticipating the play. I turned up into the hole. Craig put his head down and tried to bull his way over. There was a solid collision. I could sense that he didn't gain anything. A solid hit gives you pleasure. I remember guys slapping me on the helmet, congratulating me. I wanted them to stop because I was getting a headache.

Early in the second period, Montana tried to pass over the middle to Francis. Reasons got a hand on the ball and deflected it to Kinard, who returned it 15 yards to the 49ers' 38. We have a tip drill we practice every week. We practice it so people will react coolly in situations like this, and Gary did.

Soon after that, Simms found rookie tight end Mark Bavaro over the middle on an 18-yard touchdown pass. Schubert's PAT put us ahead, 10-0. "I was fooled," 49ers' defensive back Ronnie Lott said. "I thought he was going to run a corner route and he ran a seam."

Bavaro's nickname is Rambo. He doesn't talk a lot. He just goes out and plays. He was an important contributor for us in 1985. After Zeke Mowatt went down with a knee injury in our final preseason game, Mark got the starting job by default. And he had a fine season blocking and catching. This catch was his best of the year. He just stuck his right hand up over his head, the ball hit it and he brought it back down to his body.

"I thought it was over my head," Bavaro said. "It hit my forearm and started rolling down to my wrist . . . Phil just threw the ball over Lott's head and that was it."

Still, you're never comfortable against an explosive team like the 49ers. Midway through the period, they drove from their own 12 to our nine-yard line, where they had first-and-goal. Along the way, we were penalized 15 yards when Marshall punched the 49ers' left tackle Bubba Paris. They got another first down when Merrill hit Montana late after a third-down sack by Marshall. We also gave them a first down when Watts was called for holding on a third-down incompletion.

I call the defensive signals. I didn't say anything in the huddles about the penalties. They were dumb, but we were just being aggressive. There was 1:54 left in the half, and they were on our nine. This was the most critical series of the game. If the 49ers scored a touchdown, they would have momentum going into the second half. I told everybody to stay calm and make the plays.

On first down, Montana pitched to Craig, trying to circle right end. Banks stopped him after a two-yard gain. Then Montana overthrew Craig on a pass to the left, with Lawrence Taylor in Montana's face on a blitz. I'm glad L.T. forced Montana to throw before he wanted to because I had lost Craig. If Montana had been able to find him, it was a certain touchdown.

On third down, 49ers' center Fred Quillan moved the ball before he snapped it, and they were penalized five yards for being offside. That made it third-and-goal at the 12. Then Montana found Clark with a nine-yard pass to the left. Our right corner, Perry Williams, came up and made a nice tackle. We forced them to settle for Ray Wersching's 21-yard field goal with 22 seconds left. We took a 10–3 lead to the dressing room.

"That was the biggest mental boost of the game," our noseguard Jim Burt said, "when we stopped them . . . They had eight cracks at us inside the 20. It was exhausting and it was getting chaotic."

Dwight Clark said, "We started wondering 'what's gonna work against these guys.' It was kind of bend but don't break. We'd get a couple of first downs and then *wham!*—they'd stop us on third-and-one."

At halftime, I told the team that we should continue to play aggressively but not do anything dumb. Coach Parcells said we had them on the ropes and if we kept playing the way we were, the game would be ours.

Our offense took the pressure off us by taking the second-half kickoff and marching 77 yards to score on Simms' play-action, three-yard touchdown pass to backup tight end Don Hasselbeck. It was a play Simms had run 50 times in practice but that he never had thrown to Hasselbeck. This time Hasselbeck was open over the middle. Wide open. Schubert's kick put us ahead, 17–3.

"The 49ers looked at me," Hasselbeck said, "and said, 'That big goon's not going to do anything. He hasn't done anything all year.'" Strong safety Carlton Williamson ignored Hasselbeck and broke toward the line, expecting a run. "Hell," Hasselbeck said, "so did I. We've been traditionally conservative down there, preferring to mash it out instead of throwing."

Hasselbeck played for New England in 1980 when Parcells was an assistant coach there. Don was resigned to being retired after the Giants released him in training camp before the 1985 season. But when Mowatt got hurt, we recalled Hasselbeck as insurance. Hasselbeck wound up spending nine weeks of the season on the injured reserve list with a hamstring problem. But he was there when we needed him.

"What a cat," he said later. "I have nine lives. I'm usually the first one out of the locker room. My wife's going to think I got kidnapped. I just keep coming back—like a bad odor. My lease on my house runs out tomorrow. I guess we're going to get a room at the Sheraton. While I was on IR, I watched a lot of games from section 329. It was terrible, terrible. I had beer spilled on me and guys kept yelling, "Sit down, big guy!"

After Don's catch, we knew the 49ers would have to pass to get back into the game, so we turned our loose pass rush. We also hit Craig hard and intimidated him into dropping a half-dozen passes because he heard us coming. The 49ers got no closer than our 18 in the last period. We earned the right to play the Bears in Chicago in the NFC semifinals.

Montana wound up completing 26 of 47 passes for 296 yards, but we never let him hit the big play. And we sacked him four times. "Joe didn't want to tell anybody he was hurting," Clark said, "but I noticed it in the warm-ups. He didn't look real sharp, but he had a great game, anyway."

"We played the game with a number of injuries," 49ers' coach Bill Walsh said, "but that's no excuse. That's not to suggest we would've won otherwise, because the Giants played a great game."

"I thought our defense was absolutely magnificent," Parcells said. "Pressure, pressure, that was it. From Headen, Martin and everybody else . . . Those were the (defending) world champions. Somebody had to get rid of them. I'm glad we did."

"That was our best defensive effort since I've been here," said Burt, "because of the competition and the importance of the game."

"We were awesome," Taylor said. "We kicked their ass. That's all there is to it."

"There's a tradition of defense here," Merrill said. "And you want to carry on a tradition. When we play near our ability, this is what we look like. It was our finest hour today . . . It was electrifying. Everybody was wired."

As the final seconds ticked away, the stadium loudspeakers rang with words from a song by the rock group Queen which seemed to apply to the 49ers:

> *Ya got mud on ya face.*
> *A big disgrace.*
> *Somebody better put you*

Back into your place.
We will, we will rock you.

On the sideline, Merrill dumped a bucket of ice over Parcells' head and he didn't seem to mind. Winning is what this game is all about. You can do almost anything when you win. A fan held up a sign proclaiming "Home after 23 years."

After the game, 49ers' linebacker Riki Ellison said, "The Giants were a great team. They beat us fair and square."

Joe Morris gained 141 yards on 28 carries. He had a helluva year, becoming the first Giant since Ron Johnson in 1972 to exceed 1,000 yards rushing. It was a tribute to his persistence. He was our No. 2 draft pick in 1982 but gained a total of only 193 yards in his first two seasons, fumbling often and flubbing his assignments. But he hung in there, got a chance to start in 1984, and blossomed in 1985. He was the catalyst for our season.

"At my height," Morris said, "there's some things I give away. If you want a big receiver out of the backfield, I'm not your guy. I've had to work hard. When I first came here, I couldn't block. The second year, I couldn't block very well. The third year, I got better. Now, the fourth year, I can block." We were more concerned about his running.

"Sometimes it takes a while to adjust," our offensive coordinator Ron Erhardt said. "In college (at Syracuse), they ran Joe straight ahead. Running across a formation was something new to him. Sometimes you have to slow down and read the blocks. Sometimes you have to accelerate to get away from the pursuit. Joe has seen film on how guys were bringing him down. He recognized it shouldn't have been happening."

It stopped happening in 1985. "His improvement has come mostly in the confidence level," our center, Bart Oates said.

"I make better reads now," Morris said. "I'm more confident in what the linemen are going to do and more confident in my job. But personal records don't mean anything. It's the team record that counts." That's Joe—he's so unselfish. The linemen love to block for him.

"Joe gets into the hole so fast he kind of makes the linemen look good," our right guard Chris Godfrey said.

"He was making superb cuts, reading his blocks well," Ellison said. "He wasn't attacking holes as much as he was reading." We had to pass too much in 1984. Running Joe kept our defense off the field, kept us rested.

"We couldn't wait to get out of the huddle," Godfrey said.

"As a kid," Morris said, "I dreamed of playing college football. Never this. This is a fantasy world."

We held the 49ers without a touchdown for the first time in 40 games and held them to only 94 yards rushing, limiting Craig to nine carries for 23 yards. He caught only two passes for 18 yards. A Super Bowl star the year before, Craig ended his 1985 season battered, bruised and embarrassed.

"A lot of those passes I should have caught," Craig said. "No excuses. They were right there in my hands and I didn't look them in. How many'd I drop? Five. I think before this, the most I ever dropped was two in a game . . . The Giants are a very physical team and I have the bruises to prove it. I give them a lot of credit. I couldn't go anywhere on the field without somebody following me."

Those drops happened, I think, because we played the most physical game of our lives. "Usually," Merrill said, "Craig bounces up after a tackle. Today, he was getting up in sections."

Our offense almost met its goals, gaining 174 yards rushing, 181 passing and allowing no sacks. "They kept us off balance," 49ers' cornerback Dwight Hicks said.

"They threw when we expected them to run," the 49ers' Williamson said, "and they ran when we expected them to throw." It was nice hearing people talk about how tough we were. I hope there'll be a lot more talk like that in 1986.

Our locker room was not really ecstatic after the game. We realized that beating the 49ers was only a first step. Our goal was to reach the Super Bowl. The road is long. It starts each year in July.

3 Getting Ready

I WAS ENTHUSIASTIC in the 1985 off-season because we had surprised a lot of people—including ourselves—by going 9–7 in 1984 and beating the Rams in the playoffs. We had 22 first- and second-year players on our final roster, and I figured that they had to benefit from the experience. I had decided I wanted to play three or four more years. To do that I would have to devote more time to working out. I had spent the previous three off-seasons commuting to Bethpage, Long Island, where I worked as a job placement interviewer for Grumman Aerospace Corp. But after the 1984 season I did not go return. My first concern was my body—my livelihood.

After cleaning out my locker, I took a couple of days to relax and recuperate from the season. I watched the 49ers beat the Bears for the NFC title. Then I went to South Carolina and spent some time with my sisters and my daughter. I was reassessing the season subconsciously. After a football season you don't just go right into something entirely different. You've just spent six months in a daily regimen of lifting weights, practicing, taking on scouting reports and game plans, watching film, playing games, celebrating after a win, or thinking about what went wrong after a loss. You have to come down from that, deprogram yourself.

The six months of programming begins each year in training camp, where you learn the basics, like what defenses you're going to play and even how the huddle is going to be formed. You are coached in practice to implement on the field what you learn in the classroom.

The mental aspect is tougher to come down from because you're constantly thinking *football, football, football*. Physically, all you have to do is just stop. To some people it's a welcome relief because they're sore, they're injured, but mentally you're still doing things that are football-related, just thinking X's and O's.

Knowing defenses becomes your daily bread. There are certain zone defenses implanted in your gray matter, so that you can react without thinking about it. It usually takes two or three weeks to clear your head. But I was happy the hitting stopped after the 1984 season because it was one of the most pain-filled years I've ever had. In the final preseason game that year, I hurt my ribs. I usually wear rib pads, but sometimes I get to thinking I'm invincible. Before that game, I saw the pads in my locker and I said, "Nah, I don't need them." Then I was pursuing a ballcarrier and a lineman turned to cut me off. I slipped his block, but he fell and kicked his legs up at me. The heel of his foot caught me right in the ribs, separating some cartilage. So I started the regular season wearing a flak vest. It was quite painful.

Then just as my ribs were healing, in our third game Redskin guard Russ Grimm twice fell on the back of my legs and hurt my ankle, separating a bone from the cartilage. Two games later, I hit Dwayne Crutchfield of the Rams at the goal line with all my weight on my right ankle. A shot of pain went up and down my leg.

For the rest of the year, I couldn't hit anybody with my left side because of the ribs. On a sweep to my right, I couldn't take on anybody with my inside shoulder. And the ankle limited my lateral quickness—I couldn't change directions well. People got outside me easily. Each game was a struggle. After a while I felt like El Cid. I felt my value was symbolic. I just wasn't playing as well as I could.

I struggled through practices and the last 11 games from week to week with the ankle heavily taped. After each game, the ankle would swell up again. The only thing that would cure it was rest, but I couldn't afford to rest. That's what Bill Parcells told me. When reporters asked him why I was missing tackles, Parcells bristled. He never would acknowledge that I was hurt. He didn't want to give our opponents information that might help them attack us.

I knew some fans were grumbling that I was washed up. That hurt. They didn't know how badly I was hurting. Only the reporters who came to practice every day knew. And they didn't make a big deal out of it. When I was voted to the Pro Bowl, I asked our public relations director, Ed Croke, to draft a release for me, recommending that Jim

Collins of the Rams go in my place. I honestly thought he had a better year. Croke told me he would write the letter, but he never did. I changed my mind, anyway, and accepted the free vacation. The Giants front office thinks I'm a flake. I guess I've done nothing to discourage the notion.

After the season I had a month to heal before the Pro Bowl, the NFL's annual all-star game. It's played in Hawaii the Sunday after the Super Bowl. My defensive coordinator in the Pro Bowl was the Bears' Buddy Ryan, a super guy to play for, a lot of fun, and not really a guy who wanted to spend a whole lot of time in meetings. He just tells you what to do and wants you go out and do it. We all liked his approach. Players don't really talk much about football in Hawaii. We don't take the game seriously. The talk is about where you're going each night.

I took Terry Jackson, my former Giants' teammate, as my guest. He's with the Seattle Seahawks now. He slept late every day. I practiced. Then I went back to Waikiki Beach at the Hilton Hawaiian Village and we took in the scenery. The Pro Bowl for me means recognition by my peers. It means more to a player to be recognized by his peers than by the media or the club. Players play against players.

After our 1983 season ended (we were 1–10–1 in our last 12 games, finishing with a 33–12 loss to Oakland), Howie Long of the Raiders came up to me and said, "Harry, I've been following your career and I think you're a helluva player. I really admire you." That took away some of the sting.

At the Pro Bowl, guys like Randy White and Dennis Harrah arrive early before practices and put an orange paste we call "heat," which is used as a muscle-relaxer, in the players' jocks. I always enjoyed watching the unsuspecting dupes putting on their jocks. Their faces turn red as the pain sets in. Then they rip off the jocks, run to the shower and wash the stuff off. Everybody else is howling. After that, regardless of appearances, everybody smells their jocks the rest of the week.

We, the NFC, lost the game to the AFC. We did not have as good an offense as in the previous Pro Bowl when Bill Walsh of the 49ers was our coach. I don't remember the score. I did a lot of work on special teams since I was voted in as an alternate. Mike Singletary of Chicago and E.J. Junior of St. Louis were chosen ahead of me, so I didn't start.

The highlight of the week was relaxing around the outdoor bar at the hotel. Every year when I see Randy White I send two or three pitchers of beer to his table. He sends me back a pitcher. It's become a tradition with us, a sign of mutual respect. He told me after the 1983 season, when I was disenchanted with the Giants, that he'd be honored to play in front of me—if the Cowboys could work out a trade. But there was no way the Giants would send me to a division rival.

There have been a lot of fun times at Pro Bowls. The first one I attended was in 1978, when the game still was played in Los Angeles. A big group of players was sitting around drinking beer at the hotel bar one night. Everybody was hitting on a waitress named Donna, who had a low-cut outfit and was well-endowed. Everybody wanted a shot at taking her home. There was one guy in the group, whose name I'll withhold, who had a reputation for being an All-American Boy and a workaholic. No player worked harder at his job than this guy. He was a physical fitness nut, always doing sit-ups, crunches, and other exercises. Well, he was sitting with us, keeping his nose clean. And Donna thought he was cute. When our party broke up, she wound up leaving with this guy, and leaving the rest of us shaking our heads. We didn't know what she saw in him.

I stumbled back to my room and a few minutes later my phone rang. It was All-American Boy. "Harry," he said. "Do you know how to roll grass?" Now I was really shocked. I told him, "I'll be right up and see what I can do."

I walked into his room and they were sitting on the bed. Donna had a plastic bag full of marijuana. Where I come from, I'd seen old men rolling tobacco cigarettes, so I just put a little grass on a piece of rolling paper, rolled it, licked it, and it was a joint. All-American Boy thanked me. I could see by the look in his eyes that he figured after they smoked the joint, Donna would be nice and loose, ready to do anything.

The next day as we were getting on the bus to go to practice, I saw All-American Boy. He had this big smile on his face, but he wasn't giving out any information. He just kept saying, "you wouldn't believe it, you wouldn't believe it." He could have bombed out. We'll never know for sure. He didn't really acknowledge whether he had smoked any grass or had sex with Donna or anything. He just kept smiling.

That's the way it is at the Pro Bowl. About five years ago, running back Ottis (O.J.) Anderson of the St. Louis Cardinals and I got to be friends. It's kind of funny. You play against a guy and you never know what he's really like. You get out there and you see a different side of a player, away from the pads and the helmets.

Ottis and I decided to go out on an outrigger canoe. He invited two young ladies to come out with us. The guide paddling the canoe said we shouldn't worry about anything because they were good at it. But I'm not a great swimmer, so I had two life jackets on.

We went out and then started paddling to try to catch a wave to come in to shore. The guides told us not to stop paddling, no matter what happened. They said the canoe would not sink. Right. But just then it started to fill with water. We kept paddling, but soon it was up to our waists. Three of us tourists, plus three women and two guides. The guides told us we'd have to get out and hang on to the side while they bailed it out.

I had on a pair of $50 sunglasses that fell off and sank to the bottom. Once they bailed out the boat, we scrambled back in. The guides wanted to go back out and try to catch another wave. I told them to take us back in. As soon as we got back to land, I jumped out, dropped to my knees and kissed the sand. I had been scared to death. Ottis kidded me for a couple of years about that.

The fact that I know him well does not change the way I play against the Cardinals, whom we play twice a year. In fact, our friendship makes me lower my shoulder and hit him a little harder. I think if I eased up, he would lose respect for me. I don't think Ottis ever looks forward to playing the Giants. There are probably a lot of other players who don't relish the prospect of facing me. I remember one guy who used to close his eyes and sort of roll up in the fetal position when I tackled him.

When you spend 10 years in the NFL, you make some friends. When I was in college, I met Bennie Cunningham, now a tight end for the Steelers, when he was at Clemson. After his games, he used to come back and party at my school, South Carolina State because he had a girlfriend there. I've followed his career. You root for certain guys—except when they play against you.

The closest friends I have through football are Barney Chavous of the Denver Broncos and Donnie Shell of the Pittsburgh Steelers. Both were college teammates of mine. Barney and I were defensive linemen and Donnie was a linebacker. We had the same position coach. We hung out and partied together, but none of us were wild. We were good-citizen types.

Barney was the oldest. He was one of the first guys I met at S.C. State. His only concern when he was a senior and I was a freshman was: "Can you help us win?" He did not seem to care for much outside of the success of the team. His nickname was "Bozo" because he was light-skinned and had mutton chop sideburns. We called Donnie Shell "Neck" because he didn't seem to have one. His head seemed to grow right out of his shoulders.

The three of us have stayed close, I think, because we all live in South Carolina. We view ourselves as going off to war each year and returning to South Carolina in the off-season to lick our wounds and get ready for the next campaign. When you experience the same things, you develop a mutual respect. We all know what it takes to get through a season. And a football season is the closest thing to war I can imagine.

I have pictures of myself with James Lofton, Shell, Stanley Morgan, and their wives from get-togethers at Pro Bowls. Whenever I see Lofton on the field before we play the Packers, I always ask him how Beverly and the baby are doing. Some people are friendlier than others. I know Terry Jackson absolutely hated Drew Pearson. Every time they played each other, they just went after each other physically. Sometimes in pile-ups, players call each other every kind of vile name. But a lot of times, as players get up, it's more or less just a mechanical unraveling. Sometimes guys say, "How's the wife and kids?" or "Nice hit."

Anyway, after the 1985 Pro Bowl I came back to New Jersey and then spent two more weeks in South Carolina. In late February, 1985, I started my off-season conditioning program. I was tired of going to the stadium, so I elected to work out at a health club near my townhouse. I wanted to be stronger, more flexible, and have greater endurance. As players age, their bodies tend to get stiffer. Playing in the NFL becomes a year-round job. The off-season conditions you for the season.

I wrote out a conditioning plan and tried to stick to it. I'd start with 15 minutes of basic stretching—arms, back, thighs, buttocks, and ankles. Then I would ride the stationary bicycle for 12 minutes. Then I would start my weight-lifting with the bench press. I wanted to increase strength in my arms and shoulders. I was never really a big weight-lifter. But the more I got into it and thought about how it could help me, the more I began to like it. I started benching 275 pounds, and by the end of my training I was up to 385. I worked out every week except one or two right up until training camp began in July.

I did distance running through my neighborhood at 6 a.m. each day, too. I look at it as a part of my job. I think I worked out more before the 1985 season than I did in all of my previous off-seasons combined. I still enjoy football. I realize I don't have the same body I had years ago, but I haven't incurred any serious injuries. I feel I can still contribute and play at an all-pro level. I've just got to work harder to stay in shape.

I did only six speaking engagements in the 1985 off-season. Most were for charitable organizations. I did a football league dinner and a United Way commercial. I did a Special Olympics outing in South Carolina. I did some work with the Boys Club down there. That's the kind of stuff I do.

The previous year, I was out at Southampton, Long Island to visit about 75 children with birth defects. Some were in wheelchairs. I brought autographed photos of myself and hung out with them for a couple of hours. Most people know me only by what they see on the field. They think I'm probably a violent person. I'm not. I have the ability to turn that side of me on when I have to, but I love kids. I had a great time with those kids. It was a rainy day, so we stayed inside. The kids were jockeying to get close to me. They each got their chance.

Other voices: "I would say Harry Carson's the kindest, most thoughtful human being I ever met. He really made an impression on those kids. He finger-painted with them, colored with them. He was with them four or five hours."—North Sea, Long Island fireman Robert Wilson, on Carson's 1984 visit. (*Editor"s Note*: Carson bought 104 tickets to a 1984 Giants' exhibition game for Wilson, his supervisors, and the children, who gave him a bedsheet on which they had painted, "The Fresh Air Camp Says Thanks Harry Carson.")

Phil Simms earned more than $100,000 between our 1984 and 1985 seasons. After what he had gone through, he deserved it. There are a couple of obvious differences between us. He's a quarterback, in the limelight, well-publicized. I'm not as well-known. Maybe I'm not mean enough, but I don't play the game to hurt people. And I don't dance after I make a tackle. I don't have any gimmicks.

Maybe I don't fit the image the public wants. I'm not a person who is out just to make money. I go out for a specific reason, for a cause. Many times I'll speak at an engagement and not accept the fee. Sometimes I wonder if I should be in football, I'm so nice. I don't eat glass. I don't eat raw meat. If I was mean, I think I could be the best. But I'm not out to hurt people.

There is a side of me that's menacing, though. I know that. There's a part of me that's Robert Duvall in *Apocalypse Now*, very daring, brave, skimming over a Vietnamese village in a helicopter dropping napalm, with opera music blaring, bullets flying past my ears, black hat. . . .

When I considered retiring in 1980, I told people I wished I could have been in on the aborted hostage rescue mission to Iran. If I had died, I would have felt I gave my life for something worthwhile. It reached the point where I had a death wish. I wanted to do something dangerous, where there was only the chance for success or failure.

I take great pride on the field in playing just as hard in the fourth quarter as in the first. Until the point of exhaustion. One time in 1979 we were losing to Dallas, 28–7, late in the game. The Cowboys were running out the clock. I leaped to hit running back Ron Springs in the chest with my helmet and knocked myself silly. But I wouldn't come out. I was in my own personal war zone. I didn't want to leave. I enjoy being out there, being hit and hitting people. I'm pretty much immune to people getting hurt. I think I'd be relaxed in combat.

But there's another side of me—the shy, serious side. I did one engagement at a veterans hospital in Montrose, New York, in 1984. I walked in and I saw these guys in wheelchairs or walking with limps. I signed autographs and talked with them. I was really touched by being with these guys who had given so much for their country. Guys like that don't have too many pro athletes come and visit them. They don't have too many people come and visit them, period. The fee was $500. But just being with them was enough for me. I really didn't need the money. I took $20 for gas. I didn't feel right going there, making those guys feel good, and then being paid for it.

My daughter Aja graduated from kindergarten in June, 1985. That was a special thrill for me. Then she went down to Florence for the summer. I came down for two weeks just before camp over Fourth of July. Then it was back to work. Training camp began a week earlier than usual because we had to play an extra preseason game, the annual Hall of Fame game in Canton, Ohio. I was ready for the drudgery.

I spent a lot of time in the off-season reading books on positive thinking. I read and listened to tapes by Dr. Dennis Waitley. I just walked into a bookstore one day and got them. I often do that. I go to the psychology and self-improvement books. Sometimes I need a little guidance to get me through difficult periods.

I went into camp heavy. My assigned weight was 242, but I came in at 259. I was eating too well. I ate too many chicken wings, and I had put on some muscle by lifting. I knew I was subject to a fine of $25 per pound per day. Coach Parcells asked me if I wanted to be weighed and fined every day or forfeit a flat $250 a day. I took the flat rate. I didn't want to clutter my mind with unimportant things. I had come in that heavy in other years but I never had been bugged about it as much as I was in 1985. Doctors and trainers believe that as a player gets older he should play at a lighter weight.

I was fined a total of $10,000 during training camp, but I didn't worry about it. I was feeling great. I was first in all the linebacker drills. I wasn't dragging. I wasn't huffing and puffing. The fine money goes into a central fund, anyway. I contributed quite a bit. Lawrence Taylor contributed a lot for missing curfews and being late for meetings. But the fine money all comes back to us, eventually.

Several times a year we have team dinners, which are paid for by the fine money. I was not concerned about losing the $10,000 because when I go to those dinners, I pay with my credit card, the Giants reimburse me, and I get to write the meal off my taxes as an entertainment expense. I write the fine off, too. So who cares about being overweight? As long as it didn't affect my performance, I wasn't worried.

I remember my first camp in 1976. I was in awe. I was loose the first week because only the rookies were in then. But when the veterans reported, all the rookies turned into puppies, including me. The big dogs were in town. That's the way it is in camp. I remember having to get up on a chair in the dining room to sing my South Carolina State fight song.

The Giants were converting me from a down lineman to a linebacker. My position coach was Marty Schottenheimer, now head coach of the Cleveland Browns. He worked with me and taught me everything I needed to know. The first thing was: stay on your feet. You can't do anything if you're on the ground. You need good vision, especially peripheral vision. You have to be able to see and feel trouble coming and avoid it. You have to keep your eyes on the ballcarrier but know what's happening around you.

I learned that whatever it takes to get to the ballcarrier, you have to do it. If you have to pull somebody down, hit him in the back of the helmet, leg whip him, give ground, whatever. You must be agile enough to leap over a fallen opponent. Resourceful. Whatever it takes. You might have to grab the tail of a guy's jersey, his shoestring, his facemask (hiding that from the officials), anything.

Marty also stressed the importance of staying on the balls of your feet, in order to move into a tackling position quicker. But I'm flat-footed and it hurts too much. Marty wanted players to keep their shoulders square to the ballcarrier to decrease the possibility of overrunning him. If your shoulders are square, you reduce the possibility of having to arm-tackle. Backs are so strong these days that you really can't arm-tackle anybody. You have to meet them with your shoulder and facemask in their chests. An arm tackle won't bring the guy down.

After a while, you get to know how offensive linemen like to block you. Some are not very physical. They try to beat you to an area—like Tom Rafferty of Dallas. He tries to get position on you and wall you away from the ballcarrier. Tom Banks of the Cardinals was a change-up guy. One time, he'd knock the crap out of your upper body; the next time, he'd drop down and catch you in the knees. He was sneaky. As linemen get more experienced, they realize that they don't really have to be physical. Len Hauss of the Redskins was like that—all finesse. Washington's current center, Jeff Bostic, is an overachiever. He also likes to cut-block you below the knees. You have to have good peripheral vision, see the ballcarrier, and be agile enough to elude a Bostic when he drops down or play off him and keep him away from your body.

Some linemen come at you headfirst. Some use their shoulders. Some roll like logs going down a hill. I'd say Miami's Dwight Stephenson is the best center I've played against in the eighties and Tampa Bay's Sean Farrell is the best guard I've had to battle. Both have good agility, good strength, and love to play the game. When Farrell pulls, he likes get out on the corner and cut you. The idea is to be ready to jump or hit him with a forearm, but it's awfully tough to put him down.

When I joined the Giants, I felt like a veteran because my college coaches had been telling me for a couple of years that I would be good enough to play pro football. I didn't want to come to New York. I had always wanted to play for a West Coast team. I thought of the city as being Manhattan. I used to come up summers to visit my mother in Newark. I once saw a race riot there. So I was afraid of coming to New York, afraid that my car would get stolen or that I'd get mugged. I was pleasantly surprised by our camp site, Pace University in Pleasantville, N.Y.

We live in a girls' dormitory up on a hill overlooking a corral full of horses and a pond with squawking Canada geese. The food is great. We practice on a soft grass field lined by bleachers with fans sunning themselves. We lift weights under a yellow and white canopy. We get ice pop breaks. Team meetings are held at night in classrooms.

Coming to Pace is like being in the South. It's kind of like home. It's a college-type military environment. It feels funny being shut up in a dorm, being treated like a child at night with 11 p.m. curfews and yet being asked to perform like a man during the day. I don't think the regimentation really is necessary for a veteran, but the younger players do need discipline. I don't know where some of these guys put the food. The team gives them three nutritional meals a day. And some of them are still out at McDonald's or the Seven-11 store at night.

I try to lighten the mood in camp when it gets heavy. Like one time when we were about to get our annual lecture about avoiding drugs. So I took some grass from the field, put it in a cellophane bag, emptied a couple of dozen packets of soap powder, and put it in another cellophane bag. I taped them to the bulletin board in the locker room and wrote MARIJUANA and COCAINE next to them. I was just trying to show the rookies what they have to avoid. Some of the coaches did not think it was funny.

My place in Ossining is five miles from Pace, so I'm more fortunate than the rest of the players. Aja is close by. I can go see her and her mother after our evening meetings and before curfew. If I don't have any meetings, I can just disappear after practice. Other players go down to Foley's Bar for a beer. I don't like to hang out in town. I've never been a drinker. I can't handle alcohol.

It only takes me eight minutes to get home. I'll go give Aja a bath, tuck her in, watch television there, and still get back by 11:00.

One of my teammates, whom I won't name, was the most amazing ladies' man I've ever seen. He used to live at a hotel during the season, away from his family, which he left down South each year. This guy would screw every woman in sight. He screwed the maids at the hotel, the desk clerks, even the house detective. One year, the guy showed up at camp early. I asked him what the hell he was doing there. He told me he'd become a Christian and was rededicating himself.

Sometimes camp can be a drag. I walked out of camp for a day in 1978 when I was upset that the club did not cover my hotel bill after a speaking engagement. I also left for two days in 1984 before our annual preseason game against the Jets. I had practiced on a Monday and lifted weights. Then something came over me. I went to the dorm, got my portable television, drove to the airport, and flew to South Carolina. The fine didn't bother me.

I realized I hadn't been home in the summertime since I was a kid. I was sick of the grind of two-a-day practices, meetings, the whole routine of football. I also was frustrated because the team wouldn't trade me and wouldn't upgrade my contract. It looked like we were preparing for another rebuilding year. I'd been through too many of them.

Another thing bothering me was that our new left linebacker, Andy Headen, was chasing ballcarriers outside and out of bounds instead of turning them inside toward me. Management had decided to trade Brad Van Pelt and Brian Kelley, whom I'd played with since I was a rookie, and go with younger, faster people in 1984. I was upset at the time because I didn't think we could win with the new guys. It seemed like we'd just thrown away all our experience.

So I just skipped town. Coach Parcells, noting that I was his defensive captain, called my departure "despicable" and told the writers he hoped I was at the library looking up the word leadership. One of my neighbors read Parcells' remarks in the paper and told me about them. I told the guy I thought "despicable" was a word Daffy Duck used to describe Bugs Bunny. I knew Bill didn't mean it. He just wanted me to come back. He was trying to prick my conscience.

Lawrence Taylor jumped to my defense after Parcells made his remarks, wearing my number in practice and calling a rare—for Taylor—press conference. "I don't care what Bill says," Taylor told reporters. "Harry Carson has more leadership and respect by more players than anybody in the league." Not that I asked for the support, but L.T. always has been a fan of mine, ever since I took him out to dinner before he joined our team and tried to make him feel at home. "Harry to me is a big idol," Taylor said. "He typifies what a middle linebacker should be. He's big, he's physical. A lot of people respect him. I respect him. When he speaks, I listen. He doesn't say a lot, so when he says something, you know it's of importance."

Players rarely speak ill of those who walk out or hold out. The reason is that we all could be in that situation and might need teammates' support to win raises from management.

When I arrived in Florence, S.C., my daughter wasn't happy to see me because she thought I was coming to take her back to Ossining. She told me I could have called. I love her. A few months earlier, Aja asked me, "Daddy, why don't you just quit the Giants?" Apparently she was getting some heat at school. Her classmates were saying, "Big deal, your daddy plays pro football. The Giants don't win any games. They stink."

I told her the reason I couldn't quit was because I needed money to pay for things like her Cabbage Patch dolls. That was language she could understand. Anyway, I had some home cooking, relaxed for a few days, and came back. I apologized to Parcells. I just told him I had to follow my heart and my heart wasn't in my work. Leaving was my way of telling them I was unhappy. When I came back, I felt fresh. My legs felt great. I told the other players they all should get away for some rest and relaxation, too. Now that I'm older, maybe I shouldn't have to practice every day. Fat chance.

Early in my career, I definitely felt that some Giants' coaches were racists and that there was an unofficial quota system on our team. By that, I mean that a qualified white player often seemed to be kept over a black player of equal ability so that the team would not become all black.

I know some NFL coaches, almost all of whom are white, definitely do not like black players associating with white women. And I know some coaches just develop attitudes about black players. I'd put Emery Moorehead, Billy Taylor, and Al Dixon in the category of black players who were released for reasons other than their football ability. Ray Perkins couldn't stand Taylor.

Dixon's release was something I'll never forget. And it was a prime reason why I never have felt secure as a Giant. Al had a house-warming party and a lot of us teammates went to it. The next day, he was cut. That's another reason I don't get very close to many teammates—the here-today-gone-tomorrow syndrome.

We were 5–0 in preseason games in 1985, but nobody made too much of it. Nobody takes preseason games very seriously. The guys who know they're going to make the 45-player roster look at preseason games as a time to go through the motions, to do what they have to do. Preseason games mean the most to free agents and rookie draft choices, because they're the ones who have to make the team. And the coaches have to evaluate them.

For me, camp is a time to get back into a football frame of mind, to play my way back into game shape. Regardless of how many sprints you do, you really don't get into shape until you get into a game, get knocked down, get up, and repeat the process over and over.

It's good to feel pain, to get those knocks started in practice. But if you feel pain in practice, you stop, because there's no need to kill yourself. In a game, you must carry on. We're asked to pull up and not go full speed in drills at camp. We're asked not to leave our feet. We hardly ever scrimmage live against each other because of the fear of injuries. By the time the preseason games arrive, you can't wait to hit somebody. You feel like a raging bull.

I played a little more than a quarter in the first preseason game against Houston and never played a whole game in the preseason. It's hot in August. You're not in shape. So the coaches let you pace yourself. In the Oiler game, I made a really good stick against Mike Rozier on the goal line. I stuck him and he didn't move an inch. I realized I still had it, that I could still do it, that my teammates noticed, that it would be on film. There always is a little doubt in your mind every year.

We got a scare in the first quarter of the Canton game, when Phil Simms lacerated the pinky on his right hand and exposed a tendon. Simms was taken to a hospital and took three stitches. He injured the finger when his hand struck nose guard Mike Stensrud's helmet. In 1983, Simms' suffered a season-ending fractured thumb the same way. But this time the injury was not serious.

Neither was the one I suffered. I hyperextended my left elbow when Taylor's helmet hit me during a first-half goal-line stand. Our defense allowed the Oilers 406 yards, but we were very tough inside our 20 all day. We had a 21–6 lead with 13 minutes left. Then our running back, Frank Cephous, fumbled at his own one and Houston safety Jeff Donaldson scooped it up in the end zone for a touchdown. The last Oilers' score came with 29 seconds to play on Oliver Luck's 21-yard pass to Steve Bryant.

The highlight of that day for me was the halftime ceremonies, because I had played against three of the Hall of Fame inductees: Roger Staubach, O.J. Simpson and Joe Namath. They were driven around the field in convertibles. I was standing next to one of our rookies behind our bench. As Staubach, Simpson and Namath passed by, we made eye contact and broke into smiles.

I had met Joe the day before at the hotel. The next day, as he came around, he saw me, smiled, and reached out of the car to shake my hand. I said, "Congratulations." He said, "Thank you." Then O.J. came around and we said the same things. I remember O.J. had sought me out after a game in 1978 when he was finishing up with the 49ers. He told me, "I've never been hit as hard as you hit me." That flashed through my mind.

The last guy was Staubach. I felt good for him, because he was a long-time NFC East division opponent of mine. I can remember knocking his helmet sideways one time on a hit I made on him at the goal line. It didn't phase him. He reached out his hand and almost pulled me into his convertible. "You'll be here some day," Staubach said, referring to the Hall of Fame. After each handshake, the rookie next to me said, "You played against him?" The rookie had grown up idolizing those guys. It made me feel very old.

In our second preseason game, backup quarterback Jeff Rutledge completed eight of 10 passes for 145 yards and directed scoring drives of 80 and 72 yards to lead us to a 30–20 victory over the Denver Broncos at Mile-High Stadium. We outrushed Denver, 221 yards to 39. That was encouraging. Number 3 quarterback Jeff Hostetler also directed a 73-yard touchdown drive.

The third preseason game against Green Bay was a real stinker. Simms returned and played two quarters. He completed 12 of 22 passes for 158 yards and felt no pain in his pinky. But we lost our kicker, Ali Haji-Sheikh, with a strained left hamstring. We won the game, 10–2, helped by an 80-yard touchdown drive led by Simms in the second quarter. The drive ended with Maurice Carthon's two-yard smash off left tackle.

Carthon was playing his first game at Giants Stadium since defecting from the USFL Generals, who also played in our park from 1983-1985. In 1984, Carthon, who is 6'1" and weighs 225 pounds, rushed for 1,042 yards for the Generals. In 1985 they used him mainly as a blocker. And halfback Herschel Walker set a pro football record by rushing for 2,411 yards. Carthon was referred to coach Parcells by former Generals' coach Chuck Fairbanks. When Carthon's contract with the Generals expired, we signed him. Carthon took a month off after the Generals' season ended, then reported to our camp.

"I owe a lot to the USFL," Carthon said. "It gave me a chance to get in pro football and prove myself. . . . I enjoy (blocking) as much as I do running. . . . . I had to block a lot for Herschel because he was going for the record. . . . and I didn't mind. In a way, it was kind of a blessing in disguise. On Monday mornings, I didn't feel that beat up."

Maurice was impressed with our locker room facilities. "Golly," he said, "it's so much different here. The dressing room is bigger, there are lounge chairs, there's a big stereo system. . . . It felt good to come in here tonight and score right away. I've got a lot to prove, and they're not going to give anything to me."

We beat the Jets, 34–31, in overtime at Giants Stadium in our fourth preseason game on Eric Schubert's 30-yard field goal. An encouraging element for us was that tight end Zeke Mowatt caught passes of 40, 11, 16, and 35 yards from Simms in the first quarter, when we took a 10–0 lead. We let the Jets score 24 straight points and had to fight back from behind. Rutledge threw a touchdown pass six seconds before the end of regulation time to tie the score and drove us 62 yards for the game-winning field goal. The victory gave us a 9–7–1 lead in our lifetime series with the Jets. But who cares, really? These exhibition games don't count in the standings.

The writers provided us with a chuckle the week before our last preseason game when we found out they had started a "Slusher Fund" of empty soft drink and beer bottles for holdout Mark Haynes, in honor of his agent, Howard Slusher. The collection of cans amounted to a potential of $48 in deposit money by the time we broke camp.

Newsday's Peter King wrote a story about Slusher and mailed a copy to the agent with a plea to open up to the media about the stalemated talks. Instead, a large box arrived at the *Newsday* sports department. It contained 16 empty soda cans. Slusher spent $5.33 in postage to contribute 80 cents worth of cans to the Slusher Fund, but he never telephoned.

In the last preseason game, we beat Pittsburgh, 24–14, but lost Mowatt for the season with torn ligaments in his right knee. He caught his spike in a rut in the artificial surface at Three Rivers Stadium. The injury dulled any enjoyment we might have felt about forcing five Steeler turnovers and finishing a preseason unbeaten for the second time in 26 years. The loss of Mowatt was a tough blow. Zeke signed with us as a free agent in 1983 out of Florida State and displaced our undersized overachiever Gary Shirk. Mowatt started every game for us in 1983 and 1984 and got some votes for the Pro Bowl after his second year.

The writers almost immediately pointed out that the last time we were undefeated, 6–0 in 1973, we went 2–11–1 in the regular season. So nobody got carried away. I was happy to emerge healthy and ready to start the regular season.

We also lost offensive tackle William Roberts in camp with a season-ending knee injury. I knew how Mowatt and Roberts felt. When you are injured, it is like you don't exist. No matter how many years you've been on the team, you become an outcast, an outsider. You feel like you're stealing. The club is obligated to pay your salary for the year, but you feel like a thief. Only when I've been hurt have I realized how much I love football. I missed the practicing, the meetings, the guys.

I made it into my fifth pro season before I suffered my first serious injury. It happened in the first quarter of our sixth game in 1980 against Philadelphia. My right knee was struck by a teammate's helmet. I sat out one series, came back, wound up with eight solo tackles and four assists and probably damaged it worse. Eight days later, I had torn cartilage removed. I was on the injured reserve list for four weeks, came back, played two games, and suffered a cracked vertebra in San Francisco. The 49ers were running out the clock on us and I jumped on fullback Earl Cooper's back. My chest landed on his body and my pelvic area hit the ground. I hyperextended my back and cracked a vertebra. They wheeled me off the field and took me to a hospital in an ambulance.

I almost cried when they told me I couldn't go back home immediately with the team. The last place I wanted to get stuck was San Francisco. I had a nightmare that I'd be attacked by gays. Anyway, that injury put me out for the rest of the year. I wore a back brace until it healed.

The last serious injury I had occurred in 1983 against Dallas in the third game of the season. I went out to cover a screen pass and two Cowboy linemen hit me in my left knee. I had arthroscopic surgery to remove torn cartilage and to repair a torn ligament. But I made it back in five weeks—for our next Dallas game. I'm like a maniac when it comes to rehabilitating myself after injuries.

The toughest task a coach has is paring his roster down to the final 45. There are 90 to 100 players at the start of camp. Some cuts are obvious. Some are shocking. You can see the strain on the coaches' faces as the preseason winds down, and they make the last cuts. They also try to hide people with phantom or minor injuries on the injured reserve list, which serves as a taxi squad.

One of the toughest decisions Parcells had to make was to cut Dave Jennings, who had been our punter since 1974. The Giants gave Sean Landeta a $100,000 bonus to jump from the USFL Baltimore Stars, so the deck was stacked against Dave. Both of them were booming kicks in camp. Dave had held off dozens of other challengers through the years, but not this one.

"I wish it could go on forever," Jennings said of his career, "but it was either me or Lawrence Taylor."

When Dave got cut, there were tears in his eyes. He told me what Bill had said to him and that he hoped to go somewhere else. He told me, "Harry, I don't want to go to the Jets." They were our rivals for publicity and fan support. There aren't too many Jets and Giants players who are friendly toward their rivals. Sure enough, though, the Jets signed Dave as a free agent, and he spent the 1985 season with them. We were happy he caught on somewhere.

A few weeks after he was cut, we had a team dinner at Beefsteak Charlie's on Route 4 in New Jersey near the stadium, and we presented Jennings with a Rolex watch. Everybody donated $25, and the team matched our total. Dave told us that Giants' aide Vinnie Swerc, who has been with the team 53 years, could not come and tell Dave he was cut. Vinnie is "The Turk." It's his job to tell players who are released to go see the coach—and bring their playbooks. Then Vinnie makes their travel arrangements and sees that they are paid. But he could not tell Jennings. That tells you something about Dave and about Vinnie.

Swerc, 72, has missed only three games since he became involved with the Giants in 1933. He was a water boy then. He scraped the mud off cleats with a tongue depressor. He worked part-time for the team until 1974, when it hired him full-time. He's a crusty old guy who usually is not phased by anything. I give him a bottle of liquor once in a while as a gift. He takes care of me with tickets when I need them. He never impressed me as the sentimental sort. That's why the thing with Jennings was unusual. There does beat a heart under that rough exterior.

"I told coach Parcells I didn't want to do it," Swerc said. "Dave was around for 12 years and he was a very friendly guy. I would have cried more than him if I had to tell him he was cut. Jennings was one guy I wouldn't do it to."

*　　　*　　　*

After our undefeated preseason, I concluded that we had a pretty good team. But I knew that before we started. I saw young guys that were better than people we've had in camp before. Guys like our No. 1 draft choice George Adams, a big running back with size, quickness, moves. Safety Herb Welch, a No. 12 pick who is a hitter, very aggressive, who went to the ball without hesitation. Bavaro, a quiet guy who just performed. But I don't even remember half the people in training camp. Many were cannon fodder—bodies for our regulars to practice against.

I was named defensive captain again and was selected by coach Parcells to call the defensive signals for the second year. Our system isn't really complex once you get used to it. The defensive coordinator signals me and I relay the information to the players.

Our defense is a product of Parcells' mind. Our defensive coordinator, Bill Belichick, sees that we execute Parcells' defense correctly. In 1985, Belichick, 33, was the second-youngest defensive coordinator in the NFL. When you see him, you figure the only football he ever played was peewee. He's 5'10", weighs 170 pounds, and has a soup-bowl haircut. The good thing about Bill is that he's never reluctant to try something new, especially on special teams. He listens to suggestions. He works hard, and he's a good motivator.

We have our regular defense, which we call "stack," a 3-4-4 alignment we've had since 1979. The stack uses four linebackers stacked behind three down linemen, with four defensive backs. Most teams use the 3-4 these days. If a team goes to one running back, two tight ends and two receivers, we adjust. If a team uses three receivers, one running back and a tight end, we put in our 4-2-5 Mustang pass defense. Four of us including myself, usually leave the field on obvious passing downs. We are replaced by quicker players who are better pass-rushers or pass-defenders. I don't take it as an insult that most running backs are faster than me. It's just a fact. Platooning cost me a $5,000 bonus in 1985 because I finished second to Taylor in total tackles (104–101). I would have earned $15,000 if I had led the team. But I have to do what the coaches think is best. And many times, that means taking on blockers so other guys can make tackles.

As signal-caller, I'm like a platoon leader taking the players into war, giving them instructions. Mainly, I'm businesslike. There have been times when I've been rah-rah, if I think the guys need a little pepping up. But usually I just try to maintain a closeness there, keep people sticking together, working together, regardless of what's happening. We have 30 to 40 defensive formations, all of which have variations. Our play book is about 300 pages thick. We have code words that I shout on the field after receiving hand signals from the bench. The codes are animals, teams, birds, cities, and the like. Mustang, Cardinal, Hawk, Eagle, Zebra, Detroit. . . .

I might yell "Stack Cover Three," which means only one of the four linebackers rushes; the other three retreat in coverage. If I yell "Two Dallas Zebra," that means our opponent has two tight ends on the same side and we match up with our two outside linebackers against them. After a while, all the codes become second nature. But some take longer than others to learn.

You start to feel robotlike. A few years ago, Brad Van Pelt and Brian Kelley referred to themselves as "R2D2" and "CP30" after the "Star Wars" robots. I went to a Halloween party at coach Ray Perkins' house that year as Darth Vader—because I viewed myself as commanding the forces of evil.

Usually, I just worry about my own job. But at the beginning of the 1985 season, I was a little worried about the absence of several of our key players from 1984. All-pro cornerback Mark Haynes, pass-rushing specialist Casey Merrill, and receiver Earnest Gray were holding out in contract disputes. There are a few holdouts every year and they can be disruptive. But the biggest preseason casualty was Mowatt, who is going to be a star. Zeke was tied for the team lead in catches in 1984 and already is one of the NFL's best blocking tight ends. Zeke's injury left us with Bavaro, our fourth-round pick from Notre Dame, as our only tight end. He would be learning on the job.

The first regular-season game always is stressed, even before you go into camp. It's the game on which the most preparation time is spent because it's so important to get off to a fast start. You want that win to start momentum for the rest of the year. But you also go into the first regular-season game not knowing a lot about your opponent. Teams rarely use everything in their arsenals in the preseason. They try to spring a few surprises in the first game, something tricky.

4 Game No. 1

Giants 21
Philadelphia 0

An Awesome Defense; Awful Eagles

THE WEEK BEFORE our 1985 opener I reflected back to 1981, when a victory over the Eagles turned our season around and started us believing in ourselves. We had not beaten them since 1975. They were the defending NFC champions. They were 9–2. We were 5–6. I don't think anybody gave us a chance that day, but before the game I sensed something special was about to happen.

We beat the Eagles 20–10 that day and won four of our last five games to finish at 9–7 and make the playoffs for the first time since 1963. Then we beat the Eagles 27-21 in the playoffs and started their franchise going downhill. They have not been back to the playoffs since. We also gained a lot of respect for our team. It was all due to the influence of one person—Ray Perkins. He gave us all game balls after that first Eagles' victory, but he deserved them.

Perk was my third pro head coach. The first two were ineffectual: Bill Arnsparger and John McVay. Arnsparger couldn't relate to the players. We got off to a terrible start in 1976, my rookie year, and he withdrew, knowing the end was coming. He was a disciplinarian. McVay was a player's coach. McVay wanted to practice, get it done, and go home. The players liked that. But he collected assistant coaches around him who did not know the game. When our promising 1978 season went down the drain, he and his staff were fired.

The pendulum swung back to another disciplinarian. Perkins was like a mean stepfather. He demanded respect, not by asking for it but just from his actions. We'd be sitting in a meeting room and everybody would be talking. He would stand there, with a blank look on his face, and everybody would shut up. Others felt intimidated by him, but I didn't. I played with him.

One day in 1981, after we had made the playoffs, someone sent a bunch of helium-filled balloons to the team. I took one and taped it to the back of my helmet and went through a whole practice with the balloon bobbing behind me. At the end of the practice, I turned it loose and watched it fly off. Perkins didn't say anything. After the practice, we were all in the locker room with balloons up to our mouths, sipping helium. It's something we did when we were kids. When you inhale helium, it makes your voice sound like Donald Duck's. We convinced Perk to try some. He started talking with that southern drawl of his and he sounded like Donald Duck, too. Everybody just cracked up because it was so out of character for him. I mean, the guy hardly ever smiled. He worked 18 hours a day. The force of his personality drove us to the playoffs that year.

Late in the 1982 season, Perkins announced that he was returning to his alma mater, Alabama, to succeed the legendary Bear Bryant as head coach. The day of his press conference that December, I wished Perk luck. He looked at me and said, "One of the things I'll miss most about the Giants is you." I really appreciated that. I guess we understood each other.

Anyway, Perkins' leaving set us back offensively. We had been making progress under him. Perkins also surprised the hell out of management. "I thought he was a ten-year guy," George Young said.

Young did the obvious, promoting Perkins' defensive coordinator, Bill Parcells, to head coach. Bill was my position coach before his promotion and was one of the guys. We called him "Tuna" because he looks like one. He got the nickname in New England with the Patriots: "One day some players were pulling a practical joke on me," Parcells said. "I asked them if they thought I was Charlie Tuna—you know, a sucker kind of guy. And they started calling me Tuna."

He looks like a middle-aged former linebacker—which he was, at Wichita State (1961–1963). He began coaching at Hastings College in Nebraska in 1964, then had stints as a defensive assistant or coordinator at Wichita State, West Point, Florida State, Vanderbilt, and Texas Tech. He joined the Giants in 1981.

Bill is another player's coach, a guy you want to play for. I've been able to joke around with Bill just like I did with Perk. I call him

"Bear" after Bear Bryant because he likes to delegate a lot of authority to his assistants. I kid him that we should build him a tower like Bryant had in Tuscaloosa.

Parcells told me in training camp in 1985, "You know, you act like a big kid sometimes." I said that I knew I did. And then he told me, "don't ever stop acting that way." I can't help it. I like to have fun. Football should be fun. After all, it's only a game—not life and death.

The defensive game plan for the first Eagle game was to put pressure on their quarterback Ron Jaworski, who is not very mobile, and shut down their running attack. Of course, that's the game plan every week. We knew their long-time running back Wilbert Montgomery had been traded to Detroit in the off-season. Their best receiver, Mike Quick, had missed camp in a salary dispute and reported just before the opener. We knew their offense would be different. We knew their rookie left tackle Kevin Allen wasn't a good pass-blocker. So we expected to get good heat on Jaworski from the right side, where Leonard Marshall and Lawrence Taylor operate.

Football players at all levels watch film of opponents as an aid in preparation. You watch the way your opponent lines up, how he stands, where his center of gravity is. You see if a lineman has a lot of weight on his fingers; if he does, you know it's either going to be a pass or he's going to pull. You look at the position of his feet. When Marshall was watching film of the Eagles, he saw that Allen staggered his feet, for a running play. He was more or less getting into a sprinter's stance. When he lined his feet up parallel, we knew we could turn our pass-rush loose. It wasn't too hard to pick up.

When Marshall reported to us as a rookie in 1983 from Louisiana State, he weighed 293 pounds, eight pounds over his prescribed weight. He was the butt of jokes by players and reporters for most of that camp and did not contribute much in his first and second seasons. But he continued to work hard with our strength and conditioning coach Johnny Parker and with the team's dietician, Merle Best. Leonard was in great shape in 1985 and I knew he was destined to have a good year. He wanted it badly. He has all the physical tools to be a great pro. And his spotting Allen's tip-offs indicates he's developing savvy, too.

When I look at film, I also look at how the running backs line up. Are they cheating to one side or the other? Is the fullback lined up closer to the line than the halfback, so he can lead the halfback through a hole? Is the halfback cheating up so he can get out in a pass pattern? I check the quarterback, too. If he backs away from the center, chances are he'll be throwing to the left. If he turns and runs back, chances are he'll be throwing to the right. Quarterbacks usually spin to their right so they can see the right side of the field as they retreat. After ten years, film study becomes second nature.

Standing in the tunnel before the game, Jaworski, whom I'd played against probably 15 times, asked me, "Harry, how long are we going to keep meeting like this?" And I answered, "Ron, as long as you're here, I'll be here." We both got a laugh from that. I like Jaworski. He has class. He's hung in there for a decade in a tough city where he has been booed unmercifully.

All our preparation paid off against the Eagles on opening day. We exceeded even our own expectations. We held Philadelphia to 168 net yards, 70 fewer than any Giants' opponent gained in 1984, in a 21–0 victory. It was a great way to start the season. We led by 14–0 after less than six minutes on a 23-yard scoring pass from Simms to Manuel, an 11-yard run by Morris and two PATs by Haji-Sheikh. Twelve minutes into the game, it started raining like crazy and neither team got much going after that.

The Eagles were inept and seemed in disarray. They had some excuses. Their left guard, Steve Kenney, woke up with a 104° temperature at 4 a.m. in the team hotel. Their right guard, Ron Baker, left the game with a sprained ankle in the first quarter. Their blocking tight end, Vyto Kab, went out early in the second half with a hamstring pull. That disrupted the Eagles' blocking schemes and helped us have the best pass-rushing game I can remember. Marshall got a chance to play more in passing situations because Merrill, who had replaced him in 1984 on passing downs, was unavailable. Marshall got three sacks and Taylor had $2\frac{1}{2}$. Poor Kevin Allen.

Defensively, we did what we wanted to do. But I got the sense that it wasn't the same Philadelphia team we had played in the past. The Eagles were 3–6 in 1982, 5–11 in 1983 and 6–9–1 in 1984. (At the end of the 1985 season, in which they finished at 7–9, their coach Marion Campbell was fired and replaced by Bears' defensive coordinator Buddy Ryan.)

"Every time I thought I saw a light at the end of the tunnel," Kenney said, "it was a train."

"It almost felt like we were the Chicago defense out there, the way we were coming," Taylor said.

One of our biggest offensive contributors was Phil McConkey, our 28-year-old punt-returner. McConkey is a former Navy lieutenant and helicopter pilot. He had punt returns of 40 and 37 yards to set up our first two scores. "He gave the Giants great field position," Campbell said of McConkey. Because of seasickness, McConkey was scheduled to be released from the Navy in time to play for us in 1983. But after watching McConkey play in a Giants' preseason game that year while he was on leave, an admiral had him placed on desk duty for eight months in Pensacola, Florida. McConkey missed that season but made the team in 1984.

"It might have been the best thing that happened to me," he said of the time he spent awaiting his discharge. "I put myself on a training program, running, weight lifting, things like that, and I got myself in the best shape I was ever in . . . and I know that helped me make the Giants."

McConkey is the fastest white guy I ever have seen. He has rabbit speed. That's what has enabled him to make it in pro football, like Staubach did, after completing his five-year military commitment. He has great concentration and a great sense of humor. He and I have talked about his POW training in the Navy and the times he was zipping in helicopters over beaches in the Mediterranean, checking out women in bikinis. It sounded like fun.

The night McConkey, a Buffalo native, realized he had the team made in 1984, he cried in his hotel room. He was a pro football player after being away from the game for five years. "This is a dream," he said. "I dreamed about the NFL when Jack Kemp was with the Bills. I'd go out in the snow by myself, because it was too cold to get anybody to play with me, throw the ball, and dive into a snowbank after it. I always fantasized." At 5'10", McConkey is our smallest receiver, but he's one of the guttiest players I've ever seen on a football field. He's not afraid of anything. If he gets hit, he will come back. He's made some fantastic catches in traffic. I think what he does on the field is a reflection of the military discipline he was taught. He will give all he has on every play.

I like to think I'm that way, too. I had five unassisted tackles, high for the team, in the opener—an average game for me. I was just re-treating in my lane in our zone defense. It was not a highlight day but a solid day. Our pass-rushers got most of the press the next day. They deserved it. But it was only one game.

"It was a good start," Marshall said, "but we have 15 games left and I don't think they'll all be like this."

I went out to dinner after the game with George Martin, Jerome Sally, and Dee Hardison. It was a fun time. We went to a seafood place, Pier 17, on Route 17 in Paramus. It's a place we go to quite a bit and usually are left alone. The waiters and the waitresses know us and there's no real fanfare. The food always tastes better after a win.

Game No. 2
Packers 23
Giants 20

A Hamstring Away

IN THEIR FIRST GAME, the Packers were dominated by the New England Patriots the same way we had dominated Philadelphia. During the week before our game, we heard that Packers' coach Forrest Gregg had threatened his players, telling them that if they didn't play better, some would be playing their last game for him. We expected them to be fired up. They were.

Green Bay took it to us by running the ball. They showed us some plays we had not seen on their films. One was a flow, play-action play from an I-formation. Both their backs would run toward the tight end side. The linemen would raise up as if to pass-block. It looked like quarterback Lynn Dickey was play-faking to a back to freeze the linebackers. Instead, he handed off to either fullback Jessie Clark or halfback Gerry Ellis. Between them they gained 113 yards.

The Packers found that when they ran that play, our strong-side (left-inside) linebacker Gary Reasons, seeing the linemen raise up, would turn and run downfield, looking for a wide receiver coming across the middle. When Dickey handed off, he caught us offbalance. We weren't able to adjust until halftime, when we decided to "slow-play" that play. That meant we'd give up the play-action pass. We wouldn't retreat until we were sure Dickey still had the ball.

When teams use an I-formation with both backs behind the quarterback, they like to start running one way and then bend it back to the other side. So if I see them running to my left, my job is to hold my ground, stay in my lane, and wait for the runner to cut back toward me. It takes patience to play inside linebacker.

Most offenses are right-handed. That means they put their tight end on the right side of their formation and generally run to their right (strong) side. In our normal defense, I am our "weak" side linebacker, the right-inside position in our 3–4 alignment. That means I always line up away from the other team's tight-end side. Lawrence Taylor is the right-outside linebacker. Teams generally run away from Lawrence, so we both do a lot of moving laterally to our left. Since Lawrence is so quick, he often gets to the ballcarrier before I do. This is called pursuit. Some teams figure the best thing they can do is run right at him. If they do, then I'm in position to make the tackle if the back cuts back to the inside. And I don't have to run too far.

The Green Bay game was one of the worst we would play as a team in 1985. We allowed the Packers to control the ball for 36 minutes. Our offense sputtered. Our defense didn't make big plays. It really brought us back to reality. The Packers led 17–6 at halftime without having a scoring drive of more than 49 yards. We made it easy for them. We were trailing 10–6 in the second period, and the Packers got the ball on our one after our cornerback Ted Watts was called for a 35-yard pass-interference penalty. He mauled James Lofton in the end zone. On the next play, Dickey hit tight end Paul Coffman for a one-yard score.

I was telling guys in the huddle to be calm, relaxed, confident, and to eliminate mistakes. But I'll admit there are times when it's necessary to take a penalty. Like if a defensive back is beaten and a receiver is in position to catch a touchdown pass, sometimes it's better to reach out and grab him. Even though you then are faced with first-and-goal at your one, there's still a chance your opponent might fumble or you could stop him on four downs. But we didn't stop Green Bay. Our only first-half scores were field goals by Ali Haji-Sheikh. We actually took a 20–17 lead by scoring touchdowns in the third and fourth quarters, TD passes from Simms to Don Hasselbeck and Lionel Manuel. We could not hold the lead.

We played better defensively in the second half. But Lawrence kept alive a Packers' drive in the last period by going offside on a third-down play at our 28. He was trying to get a head start on a blitz. On the next play, Dickey passed to Phillip Epps on a crossing pattern for a first-and-goal at our one. Then Eddie Lee Ivery ran inside for a touchdown. Another gimme score. Al DelGreco hooked the extra-point try. We trailed, 23–20, with 4:07 left in the game. That was a frustrating mistake by Taylor. Without his penalty, the Packers would have had to try a 45-yard field goal. Even if DelGreco made it, the score would only have been tied.

I suffered back to back concussions in the fourth quarter. Once the Packers got their running attack going, they were running with power and authority. Ellis and Clark were putting their heads down and struggling for extra yardage. So it was more or less helmet to helmet contact when I was hurt. I knew where I was but, when you get a concussion, you feel very light, you see stars. I felt like I could carry on. I didn't come out. I've had concussions before. The thing about concussions is that you're rattling your brain around and you get a tremendous headache. The effects of a concussion don't just go away. They linger. I had occasional headaches during the week after the Packers' game.

Several years ago, I got a concussion when I hit John Riggins of the Redskins head-on. He is about the toughest running back a linebacker ever had to bring down. I got up, went back to the huddle, and blacked out. We were holding hands in the huddle and I could feel myself going out. I lost it for a second. I almost fell. Everything went black. I knew it was a concussion.

In the spring of 1983, I was working at Grumman and I started to get headaches. This was during the time Doug Kotar, our gutty running back, was suffering from an inoperable brain tumor that eventually killed him. I had a CAT-scan done. I didn't want to take any chances. Everything was negative. I was just having residual effects from the concussion, but it was scary.

I used to "form" tackle in college. My coach, Willie Jeffries, taught me to wrap guys up. But in the pros, the backs are faster, more agile, and they don't often give you a chest to hit. So you sometimes have to use your helmet as a battering ram. In a typical game, I'll go head-first into a ballcarrier several times. When you hit head-first, there's no chance of him faking you out. But when you do that, you compress your spine and get lower back pain. I've had that off and on in my career. You do what you must to get the job done. If you can form-tackle, that's great. But opportunities to form tackle don't come very often. You have to pull a guy down, push a guy down, use your legs to trip him, grab anything you can and hold on for dear life. If a fullback is leading a halfback through a big hole, you sometimes have to take the fullback on, give the halfback only one option, and then throw your body out and try to have him fall over your legs. But that's enough digressing.

Simms drove us down to the Packers' 30 with 66 seconds left in the game. A field goal would tie it. It was fourth-and-3. Parcells faced a tough decision. We had converted only four of 16 third-down plays.

Parcells had to decide whether to go for a first down or let Haji-Sheikh try a 47-yard field goal from the right hash mark. He had made a 52-yarder, earlier but on the ensuing kickoff he re-strained the left hamstring he had hurt in the preseason.

"Can you make it?" Parcells asked the kicker.

"Hell, yes," Haji-Sheikh told him.

"I thought it was a higher percentage play than going for it on fourth-and-3," Parcells said later.

Haji-Sheikh, his hamstring taut with athletic tape, took a near-normal, right-footed, soccer-style swing at the ball, catching it a little low from Jeff Rutledge's hold. It fell eight yards into the end zone, under the right upright.

"I still feel I could make it right now," Haji-Sheikh said later. "It's a tough kick . . . into the wind. I hit it pretty good but not enough to make it. I was a little under it."

It's really tough when you lose a game because the kicker doesn't do his job. But we should never have put ourselves in a position where we had to depend on him making that kick to send us into overtime. We didn't play well enough as a team to win. I had an empty feeling afterwards. You fight so hard to get back in the game after being down, and then your comeback falls short. I felt empty not because Haji-Sheikh missed the field goal, but because our defense had let the Packers get out to the early lead.

Despite his name, Haji-Sheikh is an apple-pie American. His father is Iranian, but he was born in Ann Arbor, Michigan, raised in Arlington, Texas. He has no accent. He set an NFL field-goal record by making 35 of 42 and made the Pro Bowl as a rookie in 1983. But nothing went right for him after that. Some reporters started calling him Haji-Shank.

We did not realize it, but this game was the last time The Sheikh would kick for us in 1985. He went on the injured reserve list after the game and stayed there the rest of the season.

Management pays the full salaries of players who go on the list. To qualify for the IR, you must have an injury that a doctor says will require at least four weeks to heal. A team may activate a total of five players from IR, but only if their injuries occurred after the team submitted its final, 45-player roster the Monday before the regular-season opener.

A player injured in training camp can be stashed on IR for a year but may not be activated without clearing waivers. Teams sometimes place promising rookies with minor injuries on IR, then give them a year to practice and learn the system without playing in games. The league looks the other way.

With Mowatt on IR, Hasselbeck caught five passes against Green Bay, one more than his total for the previous two seasons! He scored one touchdown and set up another. "I thought on Sundays," Hasselbeck said, "I'd be drinking beer with the rest of the country. . . . It's great to play. It's great to feel like I'm a part of something again."

Game No. 3
Giants 27
Cardinals 17

The Defense Rebounds

WE PLAY our best when we're scared. Before the season many people felt the Cardinals were the best young team in our division. They scared us. They certainly had one of the most explosive offenses, with Neil Lomax throwing to Roy Green and Pat Tilley and my old friend Ottis Anderson running the ball.

We felt that their offense could strike from any place on the field. Our game plan was to sit back in a zone defense and concede short completions. The Cardinals like to run deep patterns, especially with Green, running diagonally from one side of the field to the other. This was a major test for our new cornerback, Elvis Patterson. But our safety, Terry Kinard, also had to be awake to help cover Green deep.

Our game plan worked. We had great pressure on Lomax, sacking him four times, knocking him down another five times, and intercepting him twice. We also forced him to rush a lot of his passes. We didn't allow the Cardinals to convert any of their nine third-down plays. We held Green, playing with a foot injury, to one catch. We blanked Tilley. We held Anderson to 51 yards rushing. I felt the defense played well. All we allowed Lomax were dump-off passes underneath to his backs.

The game was even at the half, 10-10. Phil Simms' 8-yard TD pass to Bobby Johnson had capped an 80-yard drive in the first period. Lomax then found Green for a 39-yard score. Each team got a field goal in the second period. Late in the third, Simms took us 78 yards in 13 plays to set up a chip-shot field goal by our new kicker, Jess Atkinson, who was signed for the game to replace Haji-Sheikh. Atkinson, a rookie from Maryland, had been with us in training camp.

Only 2:30 later, we scored again on Simms' 20-yard pass to Phil McConkey. It was his first touchdown as a pro. "Since I was five," McConkey said, "I've scored that exact touchdown in my mind a million times. Scoring a touchdown in the NFL . . . I've visualized that my whole life."

Defensive end Curtis McGriff's recovery of Stump Mitchell's fumble at their 22 set up the score. Gary Reasons' hit on Mitchell caused the fumble. We scored again early in the last quarter, when Simms threw a 16-yard TD pass to Johnson to cap a 48-yard drive. Atkinson's kick put us ahead, 27-10.

Meanwhile, we were shutting their offense down. "They play a patient defense," Lomax said. "It was more than that," Cardinals' center Randy Clark said. "We expected Lawrence Taylor to be their big pass-rusher. But he was coming inside, picking [occupying] the guard and freeing other guys." The "other guys," tackle Jerome Sally, left defensive end George Martin, and right end Leonard Marshall, combined for four sacks.

Kinard was a primary reason Green had only one catch. "I'm sick of him," Green said. "I definitely respect the guy, though . . . I'm afraid to say anything to him on the field because he's such an aggressive defensive back." Anderson went into the game with sore shoulders and left with a sprained knee, a bruised chin and a puffy eye. "I'm donating my body to science," he joked.

Some reporters wanted to know how we could look so good in our first and third games and so mediocre in our second. "I hope we're not on one of those roller coasters again," Bill Parcells said, "like last year." I hoped so, too.

I was a little surprised our pass coverage was so good, since Haynes was still holding out and strong safety Bill Currier was in the hospital, his season finished due to a back injury. Their places were taken, respectively, by Elvis Patterson and Watts. Herb Welch became the nickel back. That term means he's an extra, fifth defensive back who replaces me on passing downs. Elvis got his nickname, "Toast," in 1984, because he was burned on so many deep passes. Watts came in a trade from the Raiders just before the 1985 season. He played free safety, which is like deep centerfield. Kinard switched to Currier's strong safety spot. Strong safety features more aggressive tackling against running plays. Perry Williams played right corner.

"You can say what you want," Parcells said of the group, "but I'll tell you this: they're covering damn good."

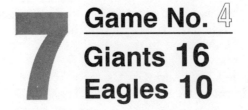

7 Game No. 4
Giants 16
Eagles 10

Toast of the Town

I KNEW ELVIS PATTERSON could play in the NFL. He stands less than six feet, but he has the quickness to break to a ball in flight and dislodge it from a receiver by tackling aggressively. Elvis got the coaching staff's attention as a rookie with a 32-inch vertical leap in a training camp test. "Guys like that make you look harder," coach Parcells said.

Nobody took Patterson in the draft because he was, believe it or not, a standup defensive end in a "wide-tackle six" formation at Kansas. The pro scouts doubted that he could play cornerback. The Giants gave him a shot as a free agent. He stuck by contributing on special teams in 1984. With Haynes holding out, Elvis got his big chance. He's probably not the type of player who will make many interceptions, but he had a real big one against the Eagles.

One of the marks of a good team is to be able to play poorly and win. That's what we did at Veterans Stadium in Philadelphia. Our offense had a bad day. But the defense carried us. Fifty-five seconds into overtime, Patterson picked off a deflected Ron Jaworski pass and returned it 29 yards for the winning touchdown, his first interception and first score as a pro. He was so happy, all he could do was scream. We jumped on him and pounded him happily to the AstroTurf.

"We did it! We did it! We did it!" was the chant from under the pile.

Again, this was a game we should have put away earlier. We had a 10–3 lead late in the game. Then Jess Atkinson missed a 23-yard field goal that could have clinched it with 7:19 left in regulation time. With 3:10 left came one of those ridiculous plays that seem to haunt us.

On third down at our own three yard-line, Simms cocked his arm to pass. The ball was tipped by Eagles' lineman Reggie White, a USFL refugee, fluttered the air, and came down in the arms of Eagle Herman Edwards. He danced three yards into the end zone and scored the second touchdown of his life. "It looked like a punt, for sure," Edwards said. "First, I thought, 'If I drop this thing, 70,000 fans are going to boo me.' Then I thought about how I was going to dance."

I'll never forget, Edwards' first touchdown. It was November 19, 1978. We led Philadelphia, 17–12, with 31 seconds left. Our quarterback, Joe Pisarcik, tried to hand off to fullback Larry Csonka. They collided. The ball fell loose. Edwards picked it up and ran in for a touchdown to beat us. Before the year was out, that one play had toppled an administration. Coach John McVay fired our offensive coordinator, Bob Gibson. General manager Andy Robustelli eventually resigned. Then the Maras fired McVay and the rest of his staff. In late February, 1979, they named George Young general manager. Young hired Ray Perkins.

When I saw Edwards catch Simms' pass and run it in, memories of that most incredible play call and fumble flooded back into my mind. It was the end of my third season. We went 6–10 in 1978 after deserving much better. And with another coaching staff, we were sent back to square one. I think that situation made me a stronger player. All we had to do was fall on the ball! We elected to run it. After that day, I was prepared for anything that ever might happen on a football field. I saw Simms' pass play developing. I saw Edwards running into the end zone. I didn't say, "Oh, no, here we go again." I had thought about the possibility of something like that happening a few minutes before it did.

I went out for the coin toss in overtime. I had called tails at the start of the game and won. I called tails again and lost. I turned to face in the direction we wanted to kick off. As we ran off the field, Jaworski said, "Thanks, we needed that." But I thought it didn't really matter who got the ball first. They would have to score. We felt we could hold them.

We did. On his own 20, Jaworski called for Mike Quick to sprint out eight yards to the right, read the defense and choose his route. Our nose guard Jim Burt pressured Jaworski out of the pocket to the right. Quick turned around 10 yards upfield and took two steps toward the sideline. Jaworski's pass was high and away. Quick got a hand on it and it hung in the air.

"The first thing in my mind," Elvis said, "was to catch the ball.". . . . The second thing was to look the field over and see where they were coming from. I stepped inside and missed one guy and broke it outside. Then Lawrence Taylor gave me an escort."

This was a good one for us to win. We were off to a 3–1 start, including 3–0 in our own division, going into our home game against Dallas. Meanwhile, Casey Merrill was reported to be in New Jersey and ready to re-sign. That could only help our pass rush, which already had 23 sacks after four games. Leonard Marshall had three more against the Eagles to give him $7\frac{1}{2}$ for the year.

Some reporters drew the conclusion that since we did not let Edwards' touchdown deflate us, we had overcome our own recent history. Instant analysis. But it was nice to hear. There are only four of us left from 1978—myself, George Martin, left offensive tackle Brad Benson, and backup tackle Gordon King. The new guys aren't prisoners of our history. After the game, Parcells and Edwards stood on the field for several seconds, Parcells' arm over Edwards' shoulders.

"You almost did it again," Parcells said.

"Yeah," Edwards said. "Almost."

Game No. 5
Dallas 30
Giants 29

Another Untimely Fumble

THERE WAS A LOT of club news the week before our first Dallas game. Merrill signed a new contract, reportedly for $500,000 over three years. The Giants were granted a two-week roster exemption for him so he could practice and get back into shape before being put back on the roster.

I'm glad we got Casey in the fold. He's a space cadet, a white guy who wishes he was black. He reminds me of a former teammate, John Mendenhall. Casey is very vocal. You never know what he's going to say. But on the field, he gives his all. He's an old-fashioned ass-kicker.

When the team threw me a surprise thirtieth birthday party in 1983 and provided a stripper who was supposed to turn me on, Casey wound up leaving with her. He's wild. Even though he was a starter, Merrill was released by the Packers for violating curfew the night before a game. We signed him as a free agent in 1983, and he bolstered our defense as a situational pass-rusher. Parcells even named one of our formations "Casey."

"Coach Parcells wants to win," Merrill said. "When I came here, he told me my reputation had preceded me but the bottom line is to do the job, perform on Sunday. They're not as concerned here with your individual life style. They give you a little breathing room."

The Giants didn't cut Mark Haynes much slack, though. Mark and his agent Howard Slusher called a press conference and demanded a trade. Club sources said the team offered him a four-year, $1.8 million deal. Mark wanted more. He felt he was worth as much as the 49ers' Ronnie Lott, who got more than $2 million for four years. As players, our only reaction was that Mark had to do what his conscience told him to do. It was obvious the club did not want to throw its salary structure out of whack.

"If you want to slant this thing, you can think that Mark Haynes is a greedy pig and Howard Slusher is the vile agent with the black hat who doesn't believe people are starving in Ethiopia," said Slusher. "But that's not the case."

Haynes was our No. 1 pick in 1980. He made three Pro Bowls in his first five seasons. He played hurt. He led by example. The younger players respected him. But then he switched agents from likeable Jack Mills to Slusher, whom the owners hate. That doomed Mark. It was a shame, but his 1985 season turned out to be a washout. And there were a lot of situations where we could have used an all-pro corner like him on the field.

"The Giants told Jack I wouldn't have to play the fifth year under my [original] contract, that they'd take care of me," Haynes said. "I went in [in 1984] to talk about it but nothing came of it. I was bitter the whole year. I played bitter. It seemed the Giants wanted me to fall on my face. . . . But I'd been on top of my profession for three or four years. . . . Now the time has come to get the fair market value . . . .If management considers me an outlaw, then what do you do with outlaws? Trade them." We all figured they would, eventually and they did, after the season.

George Young told reporters, "We've offered him a good contract, he hasn't accepted it, and we're playing Dallas this week. Life goes on."

That it does.

Young is an interesting character. The writers called him "The Cookie Monster" in the early eighties because he was enormous and always scarfed up the cookies after lunch on Wednesdays at the weekly press luncheons, when the beat reporters had their telephone press conference with the opposing coach. Young grew up in Baltimore, living over a bakery run by his mother's side of the family. He was a Little All-America at Bucknell in 1951 and a twenty-sixth-round pick of the Dallas Texans in 1952. He just missed making the final cut. Then he taught for 16 years and coached high school football in Baltimore. He has two master's degrees and is a student of military history.

At 37, Don Shula hired Young as a personnel assistant. Eleven years later, he was hired by the Maras to rebuild the Giants. It was the first time the Giant operation had gone outside the family in 54 years. The franchise had managed only two winning seasons in 15 years. Many felt that Wellington Mara let the game pass him by and was too loyal to incompetent people at all levels of his organization. Mara, of course, rejects that argument.

"From 1956 to 1963," he said, "we were a very confident, mature team. . . . We were kind of a dynasty. We were always the team to beat. . . . I felt we'd just keep on winning." The Giants of that era were not afraid to trade for proven players.

"I came in 1956 from the Rams," former defensive end Andy Robustelli said. "Dick Modzelewski came from Cleveland. Ed Hughes and Harland Svare came from the Rams, Alex Webster came from Canada . . ."

"We were a veteran team," our former quarterback Charlie Conerly said.

"We had a lot of great ball players," then-coach Jim Lee Howell said. "Just look up and down the roster. Conerly was our meal ticket. Frank Gifford was our triple threat. We had Ray Wietecha and Rosie Brown on the line, Huff and Robustelli on defense . . . good coaches, good owners. Everybody was happy and we played well."

"We had togetherness," Sam Huff said. "We were very loyal."

"The patchwork system," Mara said, "worked in the late fifties and early sixties because we had a good nucleus. But later, we were adding [veterans] to a nucleus that was already worn out. Then in the 1970s, it was difficult to build back up [via the draft] with 28 teams in the league. At least *we* found it so. . . . I'd look around and think, 'Everybody's getting better except us. What's the matter with us?'"

What happened was that the Giants made a series of awful early-round picks: Joe Don Looney, Francis Peay, Dick Buzin, Jim Files, Rocky Thompson. . . . "Sooner or later," Mara said, "the old guard wears out and there's nothing to replace them with. . . . It's not as easy as it was when there were 12 or 16 teams. But I still think it's the sound way to do it."

Allie Sherman replaced Howell as coach in 1961, and soon after the team began sliding. From 1964-1968, its records were 2–10–2, 7–7, 1–12–1, 7–7 and 7–7. In 1969, Sherman was replaced by Alex Webster, the fullback during the glory days. His teams went 6–8, 9–5, 4–10, 8–6 and 2–11–1. Goodbye, Alex.

Mara hired Robustelli as director of football operations in 1973 and withdrew from the day-to-day running of the team. But it had five more losing seasons. Eventually, Bill Arnsparger, John McVay and Robustelli moved on, and Young took over. Young had a four-year honeymoon with the New York-New Jersey media, when he seemed to convince most of them his patient approach would work. But after our 3–12–1 season in 1983, many writers felt the team was back at square one and laid the blame on Young. After five years, his rebuilding program showed 26 wins, 46 losses and a tie. Some reporters suggested Young should be fired, but Mara never wavered. He said he was convinced the team was on the right track and would improve.

Young and Parcells then engineered the major roster overhaul before the 1984 season laying the groundwork for our recent success. They weeded out veterans. They built one of the biggest offensive lines anywhere. They found more good young players with speed. They signed some guys away from the USFL. Young locked up Lawrence Taylor through 1991, buying out the $5.45 million future contract Taylor had signed with the USFL Generals. Phil Simms stayed healthy. And we started winning.

I'll tell you, some fans have felt through the years that Mara doesn't want to win, doesn't *have* to win because all NFL teams share equally in television revenue and because the Giants always sell out home games. Nothing could be further from the truth. Once when I missed a game due to an injury, Wellington invited me to watch the game with him and his family in their private box. He lived and died with every play. Mara regularly attends our practices in his porkpie hat and raincoat and is always there after games with a handshake and some encouraging words. This man cares, all right. But he's left the running of the team to Young.

The only input Mara has is as a member of a four-man committee which meets weekly to discuss team business. Young has the final say in all player decisions. But my personal opinion is that the Maras still control the purse strings, telling Young how much he can spend to sign players.

The Giants probably are among the five most profitable teams in the NFL. *Fortune* magazine (July, 1986) estimated the team's worth at $90 million, and the NFL Players Association estimated that the Giants made about a $5 million profit in 1985.

A few days before the Dallas game, some of the Cowboys' defensive backs got a lot of ink by insulting us as a team and Phil Simms in particular. I thought it was amusing. It told me that we finally had the Cowboys scared. They were insecure after losing twice to us last year and were trying to psych themselves up by talking trash.

Dextor Clinkscale called us "fakes" and said, "they're just imitating potential conference winners." Dennis Thurman said we "backed into" the 1984 playoffs, and the Cowboys were coming to New York "with fireballs blazing."

Several Dallas players also said before the game that Simms is not a great quarterback, not a winner. I thought it was all very tasteless, very tacky. I did not want to get into any verbal war. Phil didn't either. I had to laugh that one of the biggest talkers was Clinkscale, who went to my alma mater and had never been an all-pro or anything.

"I hate the Giants," Clinkscale said, adding, "They have a great defense and an offense that's going on the myth that Phil Simms is a great quarterback, which he isn't."

We felt we had more class than to start name-calling. We didn't want to give the Cowboys anything to put on *their* bulletin board. Coming into the Dallas game, our main objective, as always, was to shut down Tony Dorsett. He's the kind of back who he will fumble and he will find a way to get out of the game if you're physical with him. He's a good back, fluid, graceful, very dangerous. But we knew if we socked it to him, we might put him out. Dallas is a finesse team. If you're physical with them, your chances of beating them are greater than if you try to play their type of game.

Usually, Dallas goes for broke against us. They don't play patiently. They try to hit the home-run pass. So we were surprised when they started out conservatively this time. They nickel-and-dimed their way down the field. We were surprised that Mike Renfro caught as many passes as he did (10 receptions for 141 yards) against us. We were geared more to stopping Tony Hill, the deep threat. We forgot about Renfro.

Still, Simms threw for 432 yards and three touchdowns and had us ahead, 29–27, with 2:40 left to play. But then he fumbled a snap from center Bart Oates at our 19-yard line! Dallas recovered and Rafael Septien kicked a 31-yard field goal to beat us. Phil threw an interception in the final seconds. The Cowboys had the last laugh.

I saw that bobbled snap. When I saw the ball hit the ground, I knew we'd lost the game. I put my helmet on to go back out there and I had a frustrated feeling. You work so hard and then a mental mistake beats you. What could be more basic than a snap from center? To play the Cowboys so tough and lose on a play like that really hurt.

This loss was a crusher. The margin of defeat was a missed point-after touchdown by Atkinson, who hit the right upright in the third quarter after Simms threw a 51-yard scoring pass to Lionel Manuel to bring us within two points at 14–12. "The disappointing thing," Atkinson said, "is that I let the team down, all the guys who worked so hard." True.

Our kickers had cost us two games in the first five weeks. But our defense was not blameless. The offense had rebounded from a 14–6 halftime deficit to pull us into a 26–14 lead. Simms had thrown a second TD pass to Lionel Manuel later in the third quarter and connected with George Adams on a nifty 70-yard pass play. Our defense should have been able to hold the lead. We didn't.

Danny White passed to Renfro for a 24-yard touchdown, capping a 65-yard drive, and Septien hit field goals of 29 and 22 yards to give Dallas the lead back, 27–26. Simms responded by throwing 23 yards to fullback Rob Carpenter and 29 to McConkey to set up Atkinson's 47-yard field goal with 4:57 left in the game. That put us ahead again, 29–27. But then came his fumble and Septien's kick.

"They're up on us and he fumbles the center snap," Thurman said of Simms. "I was a quarterback in high school, and that point in the game, you rise. You don't fumble the center snap. You don't make those kind of mistakes if you're a great quarterback. Roger Staubach was a great quarterback. Joe Montana is a great quarterback. They have the ability to pull a team up when the situation looks bleak. Simms fumbles the center snap."

"It didn't matter if we beat them by 31 points or one point," Clinkscale said. "We won."

"We had 78 good snaps," Parcells said, "and a bad one." The New York writers noted that in our offense's last five series, Simms threw two interceptions, we lost two fumbles and we scored only one field goal. "It's early in the season," Parcells said. "I don't know how good we are." Neither did we.

11

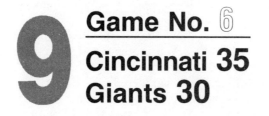

Game No. 6

Cincinnati 35
Giants 30

513 Yards and Still a Loser

WE LOST two players to the IR list after the Dallas game. Left line-backer Carl Banks suffered a sprained knee in the third quarter and was replaced by Byron Hunt. Tight end Don Hasselbeck suffered a hamstring pull. To fill their roster spots, the Giants claimed Vyto Kab, the former Eagle tight end, on waivers and activated Casey Merrill for our game in Cincinnati. During the week, Coach Parcells was upset that we had lost seven fumbles in five games after losing only nine in the whole 1984 season.

This game would be special for Phil Simms. It was the closest we had played in his pro career to his home town of Okolona, Kentucky, or his alma mater, Morehead (Kentucky) State. "At Morehead," Simms said, "everything was by bus. I never flew on a plane in my life until the New York Jets brought me up for a physical (in 1979). We went to Western Carolina one year, 12 hours by bus, and we didn't even stop."

The Giants made Simms their No. 1 draft pick in 1979, the first year of George Young's regime. But he did not come into his own until 1984, when he threw for 4,044 yards to become the seventh quarterback in NFL history to exceed 4,000. In the summer of 1985, in the right place at the right time, Simms signed a five-year, $3.8 million contract. He threw ten scoring passes and only five interceptions in our first five games in 1985. So his family and friends were anxious to see him play in Cincinnati.

"I'm just tickled to death," Simms' mother Barbara told *Newsday*'s Peter King. "It's a shock to this area that they have such a good player in the NFL. So many people have never had the chance to see him play. So this will be a fun day."

Mrs. Simms said the crowd would include the families of six aunts and uncles, most of Phil's seven brothers and sisters, along with nephews, nieces, high school teammates, college friends, and teammates . . . more than 400 people. I wondered where he got all the tickets.

"When I go home to Kentucky," Simms said, "my friends are mad because they say I talk like a northerner. I think every once in a while I become New York slick and I have to catch myself. I get mad at people sometimes and I realize I'm projecting something I don't want to. . . . But I don't think I've changed that much. . . . I'd like to think it was the way I was brought up."

Morehead State won 10 games, lost 27, and tied three in Simms' four years. And he had mediocre stats. But since his sophomore year, the pro scouts were telling him he had what it takes to play in the NFL. "I read a scouting report on me from the combine the Giants use," he said. "It said, 'a Terry Bradshaw-type. He'll probably play 10 years and never get hurt.' " So much for scouting reports.

Simms had a 14–20 record in the 34 games he started for us in his first five seasons. Every time he was hurt, he worked hard to get healthy and came back even more determined. He ran up and down the steps at Giants Stadium. He found people to catch his passes. He studied film with offensive coordinator Ron Erhardt. And finally, his hard work was rewarded. We benefited.

We didn't know what to expect from the Bengals. We had not played them since 1977. George Martin and I were the only surviving Giants from that game. The Bengals had peaked in 1981 when they made the Super Bowl and now appeared to many observers to be a team on the way down. But not on this day against us.

If anybody had told me before the season that our offense would score 29 and 30 points in consecutive weeks and we would lose both games, I would have thought he was insane. But that's what happened against the Cowboys and Bengals. We lost our second straight game and our record fell to 3–3, although Simms threw for 513 yards, the second-highest total in NFL history! It was embarrassing. Once again, the defense made some key mistakes, and our offense made untimely turnovers.

The Bengals have a 49ers-type offense which can strike early and quickly. I don't know if we suffered a mental letdown after the Dallas loss. But we ran out for calisthenics before the game and everyone was unusually quiet. When we returned to the dressing room, Parcells asked his assistant coaches to leave. That was the first time he ever had done that.

Bill told us how important it is to play well in games you're supposed to win—like this one. I thought it sank in. I thought we were ready. But the Bengals came out and ran good plays. They got us off balance, they executed and they beat us.

On the first play from scrimmage, Elvis Patterson was called for a 39-yard interference penalty against Cincinnati receiver Cris Collinsworth. Quarterback Boomer Esiason then passed 16 yards to James Brooks on the next play and for 16 to Collinsworth—who split our safeties, Kenny Hill and Terry Kinard—for a touchdown. Sixty-nine seconds into the game, we were down, 7–0. Later in the quarter, Hill was beaten on a 27-yard Esiason-to-Brooks touchdown pass, and it was 14–0. The third time the Bengals got the ball, Hill extended their drive with a 15-yard unnecessary roughness penalty. Two plays later, Brooks scored on a five-yard run. It was 21–0.

"We just didn't come out and play on defense," Martin said later. "You can't tell me that was alert, aggressive defense." He was right.

Our kicker Jess Atkinson was fined $500 by Parcells for not wearing a tie to the game. To me, this was ridiculous. Coaches feel they have to maintain order. They look at a game as a business event. To them, it is. They're like Joint Chiefs of Staff. Dallas coach Tom Landry started the syndrome. Other coaches adopted his policy. I don't really think it should matter how you look getting on and off an airplane. But the Giants' management is very image conscious. In my mind, it's how you perform on the field that should count. I'd prefer to dress in comfort. Some guys wear suits to the plane, then change into sweatsuits after takeoff.

Anyway, Atkinson's 33-yard field goal 3:15 before half-time made it 21–3. We got the ball back quickly and had a first-and-goal at the Bengals' three with 1:10 left. Then Adams fumbled for the third time in six games and we didn't score. That was a touchdown we should have had. We were looking like the Giants of the 1970s.

At least we didn't give up. We kept our poise. That's the sign of a maturing team. Our offense got untracked in the third period, scoring 14 points in nine minutes. Simms completed passes to Mark Bavaro (who caught a club-record 12 in the game), Joe Morris, and Bobby Johnson to set up Morris' one-yard TD run. Then he hit Bavaro and fullback Maurice Carthon with 15-yard passes to set up a touchdown on a faked field goal attempt. Each week we try to put in a fake punt or fake field-goal play in practice. We had not tried one in a game in two years, so the time was right. We had fourth-and-10 at the Bengals' 14. Holder Jeff Rutledge turned to Atkinson just before the snap and said, "Black! Black! Black!"

Rutledge took the ball, raised up and ran like the wishbone quarterback he was at Alabama, eluding Cincinnati linebacker Reggie Williams at the 15. He pitched laterally to Atkinson. Lawrence Taylor made a block. Atkinson scored!

"I didn't know what to do with the ball," Atkinson said. "I thought if I spiked it I might get hurt and if I threw it into the stands I'd get fined. I didn't need to be fined any more."

We narrowed the gap to 21–20 on Atkinson's 37-yard field goal late in the third quarter. But then Simms came unglued. His pass intended for Bavaro was intercepted by Cincinnati free safety James Griffin, who ran it 24 yards for a score. Two plays later, Simms was hit by defensive end Eddie Edwards on his five. Williams recovered the ball and crawled with it to the one. Two plays later, Esiason hit tight end Rodney Holman with a five-yard scoring pass. It was 35-20. It was over. Atkinson kicked a 46-yard field goal in the fourth quarter and Simms threw a 24-yard scoring pass to Adams with 1:28 left to make it look close.

"My numbers mean nothing, nothing," said Simms, who completed 40 of 62 passes. "I know when we look at films tomorrow," he said, "all I'll see is what I screwed up."

"I'm kind of embarrassed by the way we played," Parcells said. "Again, turnovers kept us out of the end zone. We didn't execute, players or coaches, nobody."

The writers wanted to know how we could give up 65 points in two weeks. I went out of my way to assure them that two games does not a season make. We had lost three games by a total of nine points! But as long as we were moving the ball offensively, I thought we'd be all right. We just had a lot of breaks go against us.

Harry

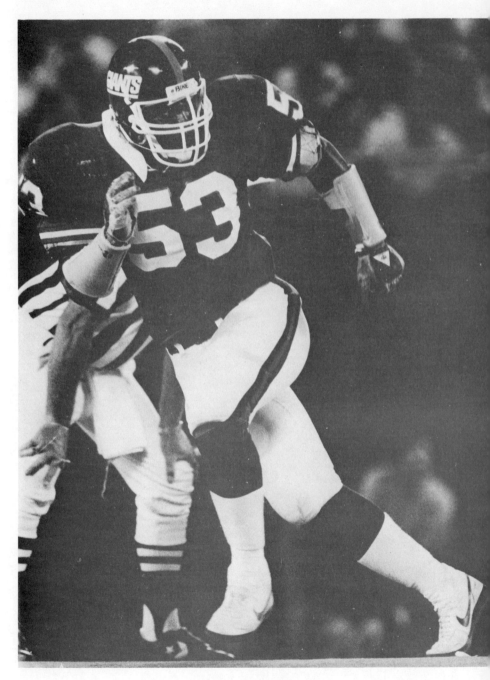

Moving to the Point of Attack

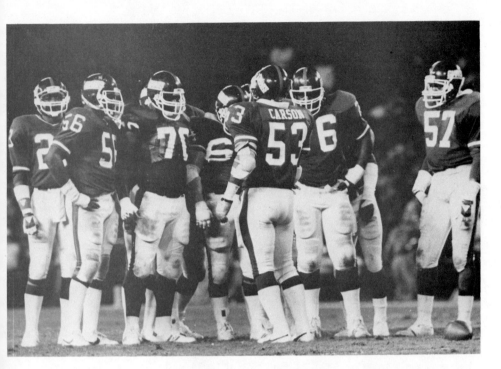

Calling the defensive signals

Carson and nose tackle Jim Burt

Lawrence Taylor on a blitz

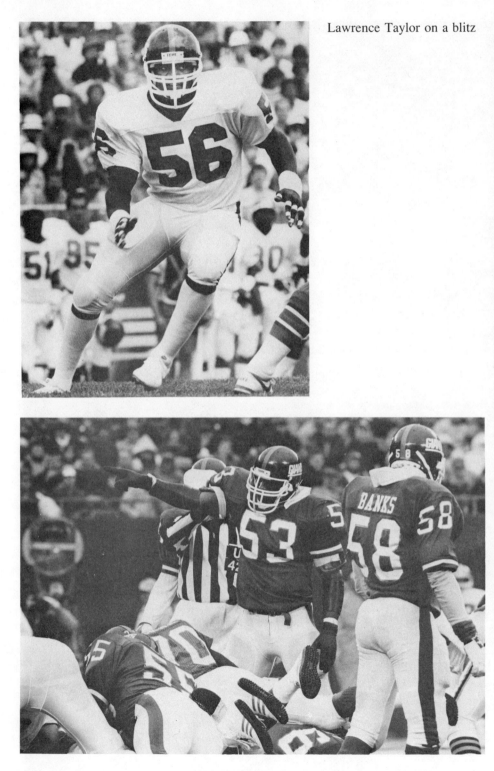

Harry calls the down

Phil Simms setting up

Carson stuffs the 49er attack

Leonard Marshall on the
move

Bill Parcells

Joe Morris   Leonard Marshall

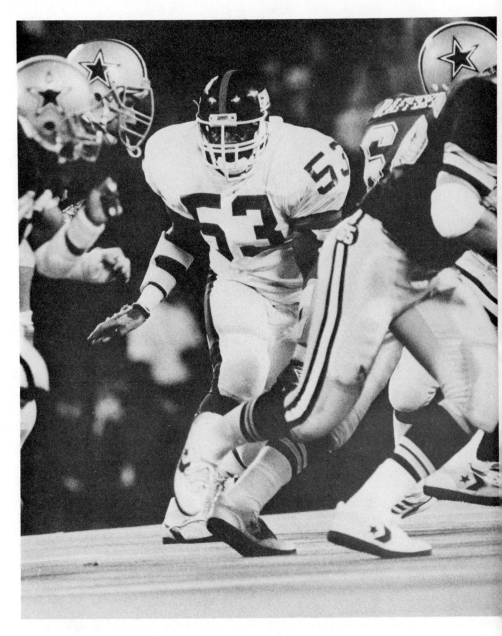

Harry among the Cowboys

L.T. stretching up for the ball

Lionel Manual on the flank

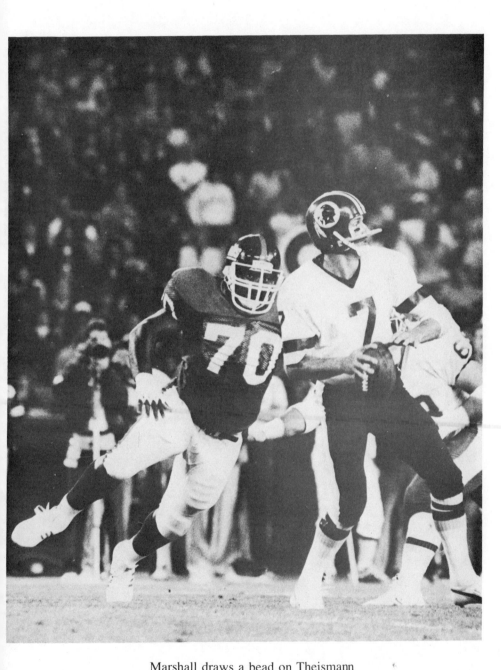

Marshall draws a bead on Theismann

Joe Morris looking for daylight

The follow-through of Phil Simms

Instructions on the sidelines from Coach Parcells

Harry considers the options

Ali Haji-Sheikh

Harry takes a breather

10 Game No. 7
Giants 17
Washington 3

Getting It Back Together

THE DAY AFTER our loss to Cincinnati, Parcells told reporters, ''I think it's a little too early to put out the funeral flowers yet.''

Of course, he was right. We knew we had lots of time to recover from our malaise. We could easily have been 5–1 or 6–0. We had committed 12 turnovers in the past three games. We had lost seven fumbles. Simms had thrown five interceptions. Simms had the best back-to-back passing games of any quarterback in NFL history—and we had lost both.

''We're just finding too many ways to lose and no ways to win,'' Lawrence Taylor said. ''We're gaining lots of ground, then turning the ball over. Defensively, we're letting them get ahead. . . . All hell is breaking loose.'' But in the old days, we were blown out every week. At least now we were in *every game*.

A few days before our game against the Redskins, the Giants finally signed Mark Haynes. I figured that could do nothing but help us. Mark did not get the long-term deal he wanted. Sources said he agreed to a one-year deal at $400,000, which would pay him $250,000 for the last 10 games, plus an option year. Haynes still was bitter and felt he would be traded. So did I.

(Just before the 1986 draft in late April, the Giants sent Haynes to the Denver Broncos for second and sixth-round picks in 1986 and a No. 2 pick in 1987.)

The Redskins always bring out the best in us. They and the Cowboys are our most bitter rivals. I remember early in my career when Redskins' coach George Allen would run up the score against us. Most of our current players weren't around then, but the memory always fires me up. Whenever we play Washington, we know we're in for a very physical game. Washington's strength is its power running attack with John Riggins and the Hogs, his offensive line.

In 1984, Parcells got Jim Burt ready to play them by having him practice for 40 minutes coming out of his stance holding a dumbbell in each hand, smashing his fists into a padded wall. If any coach ever asked me to do something like that, I'd tell him to go to hell. Parcells also rode Burt every day in practice.

"It was brutal," Burt said. "He screamed at me every minute. I knew why he did it but I didn't like it."

We beat Washington 37–13 that year, and near the end of the game Parcells told Burt, "I got you ready, didn't I?"

"I didn't say a word," Burt said, "but I made a beeline for the water bucket." Before anybody knew it, Parcells had a shower of ice water cascading from his head. That started a tradition we continued in 1985. Only after victories, of course.

"Some young people you wish were your son," Parcells said. "Burt is one of those. The thing I admire most about him is his strength of will. He's really an unconquerable human being. He might be the shortest nose guard in the NFL (at 6'1″) but he's one of those over-achieving guys, the self-made guy who had to fight for everything he got."

Burt joined us as a free agent out of Miami in 1981. He got the nickname "Sluggo" after being involved in several altercations with teammates during drills in camp. His primary task is to tie up opposing linemen so the linebackers can make tackles. He's a sacrificial lamb.

"The game of football is leverage," Burt said, "getting under people. Against the run, I have no problems. I'm small. I get under people."

Near the end of his first camp, Burt said a Giants' aide knocked on his dormitory room door at Pace and said, "Bring your playbook; coach wants to see you." Burt claims he pulled his sheet over his head. Parcells says Burt slept under the bed that night. Both say the other is lying.

"I was just praying," Burt said, "that it wasn't me [being released]. It turned out they wanted another guy."

Burt is our team prankster. He loves to have fun at another's expense. Before a 1984 game against Tampa Bay, Burt and Casey

Merrill told our linebacker Joe McLaughlin that Bucs' guard Sean Farrell was afraid of cats. They told McLaughlin that at Penn State somebody once put a dead cat in Farrell's locker and that during practices in Tampa, teammates would disrupt his concentration by making cat sounds.

So in the game, McLaughlin was making cat sounds, waving his hands in the air like he was clawing, and Farrell looked at him like he was crazy. McLaughlin claimed the story wasn't true and all he did was call Farrell "catman."

"The cat story's true," Merrill said. "I can verify it."

Another time, Burt and Simms had Brad Benson convinced that the Giants had given up high draft picks in a trade for Atlanta Falcons' left tackle Mike Kenn. Benson plays left tackle. Simms was behind a locker, giggling, while Burt had Benson going. Benson obviously was disappointed, but finally he said, "Well, it'll probably be a good trade. I think he can help us." Burt cracked up and told Benson he was only kidding.

In another incident, Burt cleaned out Simms' locker entirely, hiding everything in it. Shoes, tape, sweats, everything. The writers were let in for lunchtime interviews just as Simms discovered the empty cubicle. They all gathered around, joshing with Simms about being cut, wishing him good luck with his new team, and Simms was turning red. Finally, he blurts out, "Some guys are just assholes." Then he added, "But he'll get his!"

Enough digressing. I think we all knew this year's Washington game was pivotal. We almost had to win to get some momentum for a run at the playoffs. Both teams were 3–3. Before practice on Friday I called a 15-minute meeting in which the defense set goals. Everybody had input. Pro football players don't really react like college guys. They don't jump up and down during introductions. Sometimes you have to put a little more excitement into it, suggest some specific goals, to get a team to try to dominate. I told the team that during the off-season when I was lifting weights I set goals and stuck to what I wrote down, instead of arbitrarily lifting a weight here and there. It worked for me. It could work for us as a team.

I had spoken to Bill Belichick on Monday after the Bengal game and he asked me what I thought we could do to improve the defense. I suggested the meeting. A rededication. We had done it when I was in college. Everybody took it seriously. Some guys laughed about it, but they all contributed suggestions. I asked Curtis McGriff, our primary run-stopping lineman, the left defensive end, how few rushing yards he thought we could allow. He said 100. I wrote that on a blackboard. I asked Terry Kinard how many passing yards he thought we could hold them to. He said 150. I wrote that down. And so on.

Leonard Marshall thought we could get five sacks. Lawrence Taylor thought we could get three turnovers. George Martin said we should try not to allow any touchdowns in the first and last quarters. Herb Welch had a goal of holding them to 33 percent conversions on third down. Our top goal, of course, was to win.

We looked at the Redskins' game against Detroit, in which they rushed for 168 yards in a 24–3 victory, and they were just bowling people over. I knew how I felt in 1982 and 1983 when Washington went to two Super Bowls. They'd use Joe Theismann's passing to get us down, and when the game was out of reach they'd just run out the clock. It was a helpless feeling to be playing defense when they were just eating up yardage. We did not want them to get on a roll against us.

The morning of the game, Vyto Kab, whom we obtained on waivers from the Eagles after Don Hasselbeck went on the Injured Reserve, was in front of me walking to chapel service at the hotel near the stadium where we stay the night before home games. Every step he took, there was a click. I asked him if that was from his ankles. He said, "Yeah, and that's after only four years." I told him my ankles and knees are the same way. It's a function of playing pro football. Players have to do a lot of stretching because our bodies get stiff. A defensive back got on the elevator with us. We could all identify. We were going, "Click, click, click."

Anyway, we forgot the pain the next day. We had a good chapel service. The preacher read from Philippians Chap. 3:12, and we looked on it as being very appropriate. "Forgetting what is behind and straining toward what is ahead, I press on toward the goal to win the prize for which God has called me heavenward. . . . We talked about that before the game. It was an inspiration for the 15 or 18 guys who were there.

I drove home after chapel service, as I usually do, and drove back for the game. I park on the other side of Giants Stadium, not at the players' entrance. That way I can just walk in through the security gate without having to wade through autograph-seekers. I love the fans, but on game day I like to concentrate on what I have to do, not on signing autographs.

Early in my career, Terry Jackson and I used to go up in the stands before a game and eat hotdogs, take a walk, talk to early-arriving fans. I don't do that any more. And after a loss, I don't like to face people.

They can be pretty unsavory. I just slip out of the stadium quietly, drive straight home, pop something into the microwave and watch *60 Minutes*.

Before games, I walk across the field and check it out. If it's been raining, I look for wet spots and see how the field has dried. If it's slick, I know what type shoes to wear. We have a longer-studded rubber cleat for better traction on wet surfaces. We have a good artificial surface, one of the best in the NFL. It has a high crown in the middle so when you go to tackle a ballcarrier on a sweep, it feels like you're running downhill. But it's still tough on the knees because it doesn't give like grass does.

I wish all NFL owners would put in grass fields. Your legs, ankles, and knees really take a beating on artificial turf. There are more injuries, because people can move faster than on grass. You get burns on your elbows and knees from sliding on the turf, and they take a long time to heal. When you play or practice on grass, it's like Christmas morning, but grass needs maintenance. That means more employees, more expense for the owners. So owners prefer artificial turf.

I don't like the preparation of getting ready for a game. I'd like to just wake up already dressed and taped and just go out there and play. I'd like to wake up at 1 p.m. I don't like the nervous anticipation.

In the dressing room before a game, the atmosphere's definitely not as it is portrayed in the book and movie *North Dallas Forty*. Nobody is popping pills or taking pain-killing injections or banging their heads on lockers. Sometimes the atmosphere is like a funeral. Sometimes it's like a carnival. It all depends. Some players are very quiet, like Davaro or Marshall. Sometimes people are talking. But it's not combative.

Martin is one of our more vocal guys. He feels if we're too quiet, we won't perform. So he goes around talking, encouraging everybody. Burt starts playing the game in his mind in the dressing room. You can see him start sweating from anticipation.

Before the first Washington game, our locker room felt like a troopship where the soldiers were getting ready to hit the beachhead. Only nobody was smoking. Guys were nervous. Nobody had their playbooks open because at that point, it's too late. It comes down to what you do on the field. Dee Hardison and Jerome Sally were beating on top of each other's shoulders to settle their shoulder pads and get the feel of a hit. I was walking around touching everybody on some part of their uniforms. I shake hands. I tell them to play their best, concentrate, be aggressive, stay well. I wish them good luck. I started doing that in 1984.

One thing I told a lot of guys was that if I got into some kind of scrape—like a pushing and shoving thing—that they better come and help me. I told them if they got involved in something with the Redskins, I'd be there for them.

Before the game, I went through my normal pregame ritual. After calisthenics, I went off by myself to be alone and pray. I went to the remotest place I could, past the weight room and the racquetball courts, as far away from the dressing room as I could get. I prayed for myself, my teammates, and my opponents—that nobody would get seriously hurt. I prayed to be the best player I could be that day.

As I get older, I'm more thankful for everything I have—not just material things but wisdom and knowledge, too. I often just step back, look at where my life is and feel very fortunate to be in the position I'm in. I'm doing something I enjoy, getting paid for it, and having fun.

Every time I step on the field, I realize it could be my last time. So I want to do the best I can. William Andrews twisted a knee in a 1984 practice, had major surgery, and missed two full seasons. I'm very serious. I look at myself as representing the Giants, my college, my high school, my family, all the people who have shaped my life and my career. I don't want to let them down.

I know pro football is a business, but it's still a game. When you play a game, you don't think about business. You don't think about what a teammate or an opponent earns as opposed to what you earn. You don't think about people being cut or holding out. You think about the game, your assignments and winning. I've found that if your mind isn't really into the game, your chances of getting hurt increase. I've learned leave everything else at home. Marty Schottenheimer always said that on game day you should make things as simple as possible. Just go out and play.

We wanted to be especially ready for the plays Washington most likes to run. They throw quick-out passes to their receivers on first down. They also like to run counter plays, where Riggins takes one step one way, the linemen fake that way, and the off-side guard and tackle pull and lead Riggins the other way. They will also fake the counter play and pass off it. Sometimes they'll send their tight end across the field and Theismann will roll to his right and hit him.

I get all the information I need from one game film. I watch film at home and we watch it as a team before practices. Then we do drills simulating opponents' plays. Sometimes in a game you pursue the run so hard that if a quarterback fakes a handoff, you get sucked in and he loops a pass over your head. So you have to be alert, try not to bite for fakes.

Sometimes the Redskins send their tight end in motion behind the line and have him turn up into a hole at the snap and block somebody. The back follows the tight end and cuts one way or the other. We call those "wham" plays. If the tight end turns up in my hole, I run in there, throw my body in and try to stop the blocker. Just try to plug the hole. Now you know why body-building is important.

The Redskins also like to throw quick slant passes or screens on first down to set up second-and-four. Then they run the counter play. Against it, I have to read the pulling action of the guards and not get caught leaning the wrong way. Belichick decided for this game that Gary Reasons and I would move up tight to the line, in effect creating a 5–2 formation, so that we could disrupt the Redskins' blocking schemes on counter plays. That tactic worked perfectly and we had our best defensive game.

In the first quarter, "Toast" Patterson was burned on a 55-yard pass down the right sideline from Theismann to Gary Clark. I had told the defense to be alive for the bomb or a trick play because the Redskins had just taken over on an interception. They usually try to capitalize quickly. Incredibly, Elvis bit on a play-fake by Theismann and let Clark get behind him!

On first-and-ten at our 12, Theismann ran George Rogers for four yards off right tackle. On second down, he tried to pass to Clark at the three; Perry Williams broke it up, nearly intercepting. On third down, Theismann's pass went off Clark's fingertips in the end zone and was intercepted by Welch—his first pro interception. We got a reprieve.

The offense responded by driving 80 yards in 11 plays, scoring on Simms' 29-yard pass to Bavaro, behind linebacker Stuart Anderson. Atkinson's kick put us ahead, 7–0.

With 6:10 left in the half, another Simms pass was intercepted. I alerted the defense again that the Redskins like to try something funny when they get a turnover. They tried a reverse to Clark but Lawrence Taylor stayed at home and stopped him after a three-yard gain. It helps to know the history of a team. On third down, Marshall sacked Theismann for an 11-yard loss and they had to punt.

The Redskins got the ball back once more before the half ended, but Williams intercepted Theismann's Hail Mary pass at our six on the final play. The mood in our dressing room at halftime was upbeat because we felt like we had taken their best shots and repelled everything. We did not make adjustments. We stuck to the game plan. We told ourselves to go out and put them away.

We started the second half by driving 80 yards to score, controlling the ball for almost six minutes. George Adams was booed by the crowd when he came out in our goal-line offense on second-and-goal at the two. But he followed Maurice Carthon off right tackle into the end zone and spiked the ball with a vengeance. Atkinson's PAT made the score 14–0.

"I expected those boos," Adams said, "and they fired me up so much that I wanted to show those fans and the coaches that I'm not a fumbler. I felt real good when I went in for that touchdown. Chills came all over my body, because I knew I was in the end zone and didn't spike it."

George had dropped the ball after he scored but I made him pick it up and spike it for the benefit of the fans. "I darn near busted it," Adams said, "I slammed it so hard."

I felt good Adams got the monkey off his back. He had wandered over to my locker and sat down during the week. I call him "Little Kid" because he looks like one. I think he came into the league a little in awe of me, just like I did with some veterans ten years ago. He had read about me and seen me on television. He respects my opinions. I told Adams back in training camp that I thought he had the potential to be a 1,000-yard rusher. This week I just talked to him about not letting things get to him and taking advantage of opportunities. I told him to keep looking forward and not to worry about what's happened. It seemed to sink in.

It's nice to play defense with a lead and it's nice to play defense when your offense moves the ball and gives you a chance to rest. The next two Washington series ended with a punt and an interception by Kinard in the end zone. It seemed to me that Theismann did not have the same zip on the ball that he had in the past.

In the fourth quarter, we drove 50 yards and settled for Atkinson's 47-yard field goal. It was 17–0. We wanted a shutout badly. But Washington drove from their 33 to our 13. A pair of sacks by Andy Headen and Sally moved the Redskins back to the 30. They got a 47-yard field goal by Mark Moseley, but that's all. We held them to only 69 yards rushing. We sacked Theismann seven times. We intercepted him three times.

I was a sacrificial lamb. Reasons and I had to give ourselves up on obvious running downs, trying to knock their blockers down and make their running backs get yardage on their own. We did the same thing in 1984 against Washington. I was credited with only one unassisted tackle and one assist. Taylor had an amazing 11 solos and two sacks. But my teammates knew my role was as important as Taylor's. "Harry was putting his shoulder in their facemasks and his forearm in their sternums,'' Casey Merrill said. "He was taking on their lead blockers, him and Jimmy Burt. They stopped the run at the point of attack. That put Washington in second- and third-and-long. They had to pass. We took them out of their game plan. We dictated to them. When we knew they were going to pass, we turned our pass-rush loose.''

"Harry's our emotional leader,'' Merrill added. "He leads by example. He played hurt last year. This year he's taken a big leadership role. He held a meeting with the defense and told us the importance of coming out of the gate quicker. We didn't give up any early scores today and we were in the driver's seat.''

"Obviously,'' Redskins' guard Ken Huff said, "Carson studies his opponents. He's a very intelligent player. We run a play where the off guard comes around [a counter play]. He read it very well. He stepped up in the hole. Before I'd come around, he was right up in there. If the defensive line's doing its job, the play's got problems.''

Merrill said of Washington, "They just got out-executed at the point of attack. Harry, Jim Burt, and Curtis McGriff two-gapped 'em.'' The term "two-gap" refers to the space on either side of an opponent. Merrill meant we were pushing a blocker one way or the other so somebody else could make a tackle.

Before the game, Taylor told TV color man John Madden, the former Raiders' coach, that he was going to play the game of his life. He did. Lawrence had been criticized in the press for being invisible in some games. It's like Bobby Orr was in hockey. Orr was so good that if he didn't get two goals and three assists a game, fans wondered what was wrong. If Lawrence doesn't get three sacks, the fans think he's dogging it. Lawrence revolutionized the position of outside linebacker when he joined us as a No. 1 pick from North Carolina in 1981. At 6'3", 240 pounds, he is quick enough to elude an offensive tackle and sack a quarterback, fast enough to cover a wide receiver downfield, and strong enough to stop a fullback cold at the line of scrimmage. A hybrid.

Teams soon realized they couldn't leave their left offensive tackles naked. Taylor would just loop around them, overpower a smaller running back, and get to the quarterback. He had $37\frac{1}{2}$ sacks in his first four pro seasons. If a team switched its tight end to the left side of their formation to block Lawrence, he would automatically shift to his left side and line up outside their naked right tackle. It was a chess game. Some teams started using a tight end on each side, going with one back. Then Lawrence would wait, read the play, pick a hole, and rush inside.

When Taylor arrived, the Giants already had one of the best linebacker corps in the NFL with myself, Brad Van Pelt, and Brian Kelley.

But with Taylor we became even better. Lawrence's arrival took pressure off me. The fans watched him so much that if I missed a tackle, nobody seemed to remember it.

Lawrence and I quickly got wired in on the field. We began playing off each other, almost telepathically. For instance, if I'm covering a back and he's covering a wide receiver and the receiver breaks over the middle, we switch men. But overall, his position allows him to freelance. I'm required to play more under control. I have to be patient. If the ball is handed off, I have to wait and watch for a cutback. If it's tossed outside, I can take off and pursue hard.

Anyway, Taylor, myself, Van Pelt, and Kelley incorporated a few years ago and had photos of ourselves in hardhats on an earth-moving vehicle. We called ourselves "The Crunch Bunch" and "The Board of De-Wreckers" and made some money from the sale of posters. Then Brad and Brian got traded after the 1983 season and the firm was dissolved.

Lawrence is the most gifted linebacker I've ever seen. He makes up for mental mistakes with his great speed. He's a super athlete. He always has been a party person, but his remarks to the press after the Washington game really surprised me.

"I prepared well," Taylor said, "got some sleep and didn't go to the bars as much as usual. My wife and a friend [former North Carolina teammate Paul Davis] told me I wasn't playing the way I used to play. That really struck home."

Lawrence had had a real good week of practice, showing a lot of concentration. He had input into how we were going to run things. He vocalized what he thought he could do and what he wanted to do. He really dedicated himself to football. But his remarks would do little for his image or endorsement prospects.

We did not know at the time that he was battling a cocaine addiction problem that would land him in a Texas drug rehabilitation clinic for more than a month after the Pro Bowl. Lawrence did not confide in me or any of us, so we could not help him. Maybe I'm naive, but I had no idea he was in such big trouble. Lawrence is an erratic person. He goes from one extreme to the other. At times, he can be very cold with fans and short with people in general. But I've also seen him be generous, giving, and patient. During the 1985 season, there were times when I perceived that Lawrence really did not care about football, that he would have preferred being somewhere else. But he never talked to me about his problems. He knows how I am. I would not have approved of drug use. Not even his closest friends knew about his troubles. He did it underground.

(On March 20, 1986, Taylor released a statement confirming that he was undergoing treatment for "substance abuse" and said, "I will make the most determined effort of my career to restore [his] image." Taylor attended the Giants' veterans' minicamp in May but refused comment to reporters.

Taylor was not fined or suspended by the Giants or the NFL because he voluntarily sought help.)

I may be naive, but I really think the drug problem is blown out of proportion as far as the NFL is concerned. I have seen marijuana once since I've been in the league. One time at a Pro Bowl, as I discussed above, a player picked up a waitress who had grass. It was no big deal.

I don't know whether a drug culture exists on the Giants. Maybe I'm considered such a Goody Two Shoes that my teammates realize I would not approve, so they don't use drugs around me. But I've never seen anybody nod out at a meeting. I've never seen a teammate buy drugs. I've never seen anybody use drugs. I've never been offered drugs. I've never had anybody come to me and say, "I'm hooked; what should I do?"

There's no doubt that drugs are a problem in all walks of life, though, not just professional sports. It's just that we are under a microscope because we're supposed to be role models for youths. At the National Scouting Combine workouts in New Orleans in January, 1986, 54 college seniors tested positive for marijuana use, and cocaine was detected in three players. The Denver Broncos said they would remove the names of the 57 players from their draft boards.

"Why invite trouble?" Bronco coach Dan Reeves said.

Besides Taylor, the only teammate I know for a fact was treated for drug abuse was Malcolm Scott, a second-year tight end who was released in camp in 1984 after traces of drugs showed up in his urine. Giants sources say coach Parcells spent six days of his vacation in the spring of 1984 baby-sitting Scott, and the team spent more than $30,000 to help him. The same sources said the Giants took care of 51 unpaid parking tickets and $13,000 worth of Scott's reported debts to drug dealers. During the 1984 season, Scott's agent called the Giants and reported that Scott was "clean." But subsequent urinalysis tests showed he wasn't. It was a sad story.

Other Giants' sources said that at a 1982 Giants' minicamp, eight of 42 rookies tested positively for drugs. In 1984, sources said, a Giant defensive back previously known to be a habitual marijuana smoker was tested seven times during the season and came up negative each time.

Club sources say that when we went 1–10–1 in our last 12 games in 1983, drug abuse was a contributing factor. "I can show you in the films,'' a source said, referring to players' diminished performances. I don't know what he's talking about, but then I didn't want to know.

I know on some NFL teams, coaches use fear of exposure as leverage to motivate players to play harder and to stop using drugs. "The more you find out," a Giants' club official said, "the better it is. . . . You use it as leverage." But I know of no such tactics being used by the Giants.

The only exposure to drugs I've had in my career has been to mild pain-killers like Darvon, Emperin, and codeine. I have taken them periodically to mask the pain of a sprained ankle. I have taken a shot of cortisone in my toe or novacaine in my finger after they were knocked out of place. But that's it.

My only firsthand knowledge of drugs is that in my rookie year, I remember some Giants taking what appeared to be amphetamines— ''bennies''—before a game. I remember seeing a lot of the guys who took these pills running down under the opening kickoff faster than I'd ever seen them run in practice. There were only three or four of them. They didn't last long, and I never asked what they took. I know it was reported in 1984 that nine of our players were spot-checked during the season for the presence of drugs in their systems. But I wasn't and I don't know who was.

Once in a while coaches pressure players to play hurt. But I've never heard a coach order a player to take a pain-killing injection. I know in 1984, Parcells virtually told me I could not have a week off to let my rib and ankle injuries heal. He told me I was too valuable on the field. That I had to play the best I could. He told me he looked at me as a leader and my presence on the field was important.

I'd say Van Pelt probably was the guy who could tolerate more pain than any teammate I've ever had. He would get knocked silly out there. His eyes would be rolling back in his head. He looked like he was about to collapse, and he stayed out there, trying, playing, making tackles. Van Pelt's eyes told you what day it was. He and Kelley used to go out partying Sunday nights after games. On Mondays, Brian always looked fit as a fiddle, but Brad's eyes were bloodshot. He always came in smelling like vodka. It was coming out of his pores.

I could never drink with them. I don't have the tolerance. One time, I think it was in 1978, the Giants had an off-season minicamp in Mexico City. You couldn't drink the water, so you either had to drink soda or beer from cans. It was my first trip out of the country. I was in a partying frame of mind. The weather was humid. And one day after practice, my roommate Gordon Bell challenged me to a beer-drinking contest.

I got a glass and chugged some down. It really didn't affect me so I figured I'd keep going. Somebody else challenged me. And somebody after that. I don't know how much beer I wound up consuming. But I know by the end of the evening, I stumbled back to my room, called the woman I was dating back in New York and was just laughing over the phone. She got a big kick out of it because it was so unlike me.

There always are a lot of rumors about NFL players gambling on games. Paul Hornung and Alex Karras were suspended for gambling in the 1960s. Art Schlichter of the Colts was suspended a few years ago after admitting to several hundred thousand dollars worth of sports gambling debts. The NFL was investigating in the spring of 1986 reports that receiver Irving Fryar and others on the New England Patriots bet on games in 1985. But I never have heard a player place a bet. And I don't think players pay much attention to the point spread.

I think the NFL's public disapproval of gambling is hypocritical, since it publishes extensive injury reports each week that serve as betting tools. And the NFL never seems to raise its voice to disapprove of the publication of lines in the paper. I've never placed a bet with a bookie on anything. I wouldn't know how. And I don't know of any teammates ever having relayed injury information to gamblers.

But I'm getting carried away with all this stuff about drugs, booze, and gambling. Anyway, Lawrence Taylor certainly looked like the Lawrence Taylor of old against Washington, especially against its running attack.

To beat the Redskins, our first task always is to stop the running game. We have a lot of respect for Riggins. I've played against him a lot of years. He's not going to run around you. He runs over you. That's why they call him "The Diesel." You have to take it like a man. Either you're going to get cleat marks on your chest and a concussion or you're going to stop him. That's the kind of challenge I like: power against power. There have been times when he's hit me that he's bent me back. And there are times I've hit him and bent him back.

We held Riggins to 35 yards on 11 carries and George Rogers to 25 yards on six carries. Rogers gave me some grudging praise. "He doesn't have much speed," Rogers said. "He relies on quickness. But I respect him a lot. He and L.T. probably are the best two linebackers in the game."

Riggins said, "Carson doesn't try to go out and deliberately hurt somebody. He just goes out and does what he has to do. He's got to be one of the top inside linebackers in the league."

"I've always liked Harry," Riggo said. "I think he's everything a linebacker's all about in the modern era. I've played against a lot of them and he's certainly been as good as there is. When he's playing, it's always fun to be on the field. I like to play against people of his caliber—so I can find out what I'm all about."

"He's not going to run around a block," tackle Russ Grimm said. "He's just going to squat in there and take it on."

It's nice to hear things like that. I've never developed a relationship of hate with anybody—on or off the field. There are certain players I have to keep an eye on, though. Like Mark May, a Redskins' lineman. He's one of those guys who if you're standing around a pile, will knock you into it. He'll hit you when your back is turned. He's a cheap-shot artist. John Frank of the 49ers is another guy I'd put in that category. He likes to block you after the whistle. He doesn't have much talent, but he has a big heart.

Drew Pearson, the Cowboys' receiver, was cocky. You don't mind that. You look at players as being human, with emotions, feelings, and families at home, not little X's and O's. Sometimes, though, emotions flare. Sometimes guys curse each other out in piles or get themselves up by using a fallen player as a crutch. Sometimes guys call each other names like asshole or son of a bitch. The intensity of the action sometimes causes even the sanest players to lose their cool.

Kenny Hill was fined $300 by the NFL for kneeing Washington's Greg Williams in the facemask on a kickoff return. Hill, an articulate Yale man who rarely loses his temper, was penalized 15 yards and ejected after the play, which occurred in the second quarter, right after we scored. Kenny felt the Redskins were blocking him after the whistle had blown. After being kicked out, he went to the sidelines and started to sulk. Now he was helpless. There was nothing he could do.

At halftime, Hill came inside and was kicking chairs around in our meeting room. I went in and calmed him down. I told him that even though he was out of the game, he should keep his eyes open and help Herb Welch, who had replaced him. I asked coach Parcells to go in and say something to Kenny and he did.

"In the heat of battle," Hill said later, "you sometimes do things you shouldn't. I did something that was uncalled for. I kneed him in the face; I kicked him in the face. It wasn't very good judgment on my part."

Kenny's penalty also gave the Redskins the ball at our 50. They were able to move to the 35, but Moseley missed on a 52-yard field goal try. I always stress to the team that dumb penalties can help our opponents put points on the board.

In the fourth quarter, McGriff came up to me and said, "This is the way it should be every week." Martin came over and said the same thing. After the game, Parcells told us we had talent and had to use it and believe in ourselves. After the coach had his say, I asked him to leave for a minute and presided over another short meeting. I told the guys we can play this way every week, as long as we eliminate the mistakes. George and I thought this was the most talented team we ever had, so it was time we reached our potential.

11 Game No. 8

Giants 21
New Orleans 13

The Running Attack Blossoms

THE SAINTS never have had a winning season and never have made the playoffs. So we certainly did not expect them to beat us, even though we were playing in the Superdome in New Orleans. Of course, our history is that we let down against teams like the Saints.

I think it's human nature that our players study harder and are more intense when we play a team like Washington, Dallas, Miami, Pittsburgh, or San Francisco. Players are scared of being embarrassed, of being injured, or worried about going up against an all-pro. But when you play a team like the Saints, you think the other guys should be worried about *you*. They are. And they usually play harder as a result.

We remembered that the Saints beat us 10–6, at Giants Stadium in the last regular-season game in 1984; it was one of the worst football games ever played. That should have been motivation to be prepared for a tough game. But we also knew the Saints had lost the previous week to Atlanta, which had not won a game before that.

Our game plan focused on stopping the New Orleans running game because their receiver corps was one of the worst in the NFL. They came into our game with a total of only 34 catches. We were more concerned about stopping their tight end, Hoby Brenner, who had become quarterback Dave Wilson's favorite target.

Earl Campbell had rejoined his former coach, Bum Phillips, but he was not the same running back who had averaged more than 1,600 yards rushing per season from 1978-1981 with Phillips in Houston. The

Saints seemed to be going to Earl now only as a last resort. We were more conscious of Hokie Gajan, a slashing running back, and Wayne Wilson, their all-purpose back. The Saints ran a more complicated offense than the Redskins did in 1985. They gave us more to think about. Gary Reasons and I would not be walking up to the line of scrimmage this week. We'd be sitting back, reading and reacting. We did not want to get sucked in by play-fakes. Playing in the Superdome is different than playing outside. It's harder for offenses to hear the quarterback's signals and it's harder for my teammates to hear my calls on defense. The crowd noise muffles everything.

New Orleans is a great party city—which is why coach Parcells told us to avoid the French Quarter. Bourbon Street has won a lot of games for the Saints. He did not want us sightseeing. We did not have much time for that, anyway. We had from 3 to 9 p.m. on Saturday free, then had to be back for a team meeting. Then we had another hour before curfew at 11.

I don't like hotels. The less time I spend in them, the better. But some guys like them. Rob Carpenter has two kids. He told me he couldn't wait to get to New Orleans so he could get away from them for a little while.

One time we were at a New Jersey hotel the night before a home game and a friend introduced me to a woman over the phone. I invited her to the hotel for a drink. I envisioned a beautiful young lady with long hair, very sexy. She knocked and I flung the door open, saying "Mar . . . go." She was short, fat, and ugly. That was the last time I ever had a blind date.

We have a rule that the hotel bar is off-limits to players. And if we're on the road and at a bar and a coach walks in, the coach leaves. Conversely, if a coach is somewhere and a player walks in, the player is supposed to leave. Then nobody has anything on anybody else.

When the bus driver was taking us from the airport to our hotel, he told us, "We've been waiting for you; the French Quarter is waiting for you." But most of the players listened to Parcells and stayed out of trouble. I went out to Popeye's, a fast-food chicken restaurant, with Bobby Johnson and Tony Galbreath. We brought back some chicken to our rooms and avoided the city's distractions. Other players went out to restaurants. Nobody broke curfew. Nobody was fined. We're a pretty dull team.

The next day, we started slowly. We led by only 7–3 after three quarters. New Orleans drove 61 yards to score on its first series with a 33-yard field goal by Morten Andersen. That woke us up. The first three times we had the ball, we punted, lost the ball on Phil Simms' fumble at the Saints' two, and Atkinson missed a 39-yard field goal. Finally, Simms finished a 31-yard drive with a six-yard scoring pass to Bobby Johnson. Atkinson kicked the PAT and we led, 7–3. Elvis Patterson had set it up with a 24-yard interception return to the 31.

We came in at halftime and some guys were really upset. McGriff and Leonard Marshall were keyed up because their families and relatives were in the stands. Leonard had played at LSU and Curtis at Alabama. So they wanted to do well in front of their folks.

"What I want in life," Marshall said, "is what everybody else wants. The nice cars, the Rolex watches, the whole nine yards. . . . What I'd really like this year is to take my mother and father to Hawaii for the Pro Bowl." (He didn't know it then, but he would get that chance.)

Our defense was solid in the third period, but the offense couldn't get out of its own way. It ran out of downs at the Saints' 35. On its next series, Atkinson missed a 42-yard field goal. Our next three drives ended at the Saints' 45, 32 (another Simms fumble), and 47.

"We weren't disheartened," our left offensive tackle Brad Benson said. "It was like having the fish on the hook and losing him. When the fish stop biting, you stop fishing. But the fish were still biting."

The Saints spent most of their week preparing to defend against what they thought would be a Simms aerial circus. But Parcells elected to keep the ball on the ground. Early in the last quarter, the Saints moved into position for Andersen's 43-yard field goal. That cut our lead to 7–6. Finally, good things happened for us. After busting our butts all day and getting very little, the Saints handed us two touchdowns. First, Carl Roaches fumbled a punt return at his 12, and Patterson recovered to set up Joe Morris' five-yard scoring run. Atkinson's kick made it 14–6.

Then Marshall made the first interception of his career, deflecting and then catching a Wilson pass at the Saints' 22. It had to be a thrill for Leonard. All his family and friends were at our hotel Saturday night. Now they saw him make a great play. Six plays later, Morris scored from one yard out. We led, 21–6, with 1:54 left in the game. That made a 17-yard scoring pass from Wilson to Eric Martin meaningless.

We put Brenner out of the game early with an ankle injury, which hurt New Orleans' passing game. The Saints ran the ball pretty well in the second half with Campbell, but he took a tremendous beating. I got an Earl Campbell souvenir in the third quarter. The Saints ran a sweep and our helmets met at the corner. My helmet slid up and the facemask cut me above my eye. And I got a sore neck from the collision.

I felt good about my effort in the game. I gave Jim Burt a couple of calls that enabled him to penetrate gaps and make tackles in the backfield. Jim was shooting a gap to the side I told him and a few times he met the ballcarrier perfectly. We gambled and it worked. I love Burt. He plays a thankless position. His job is to give himself up so the linebackers can make tackles. But he also runs people down himself.

I look at Gary Reasons as a bigger, younger Brian Kelley, whom he replaced next to me at inside linebacker. Reasons has a great football mind and plays excellent zone defense. He's not the quickest guy in the world but his strong suit is retreating into zone coverage to cover receivers.

Our offense was encouraged that we rushed 49 times for 234 yards and controlled the ball almost 36 minutes. Morris gained 104 yards and Adams had 89. It's a little hard to breathe in the Superdome because it's poorly ventilated. I think our players were in better condition than the Saints and handled it better. Late in the game, once we started running the ball well, you could see the Saints' defenders getting tired.

"It's got to be our best overall day [rushing] since I've been here," said Ron Erhardt, our offensive coordinator.

Parcells said, "I thought Morris ran his gluteus maximus off. So did Adams."

"It was so impressive to me," Simms said. "I liked just handing the ball off and watching it. I'd venture to say it's the best the Saints have ever seen."

"I wanted to run it all day," guard Billy Ard said.

I was really impressed with Morris. When I first met him, I didn't think he could get the job done because of his size. But in 1985 watching him cut up into a hole, wriggle free from a tackler, and earn that extra yardage was impressive. He has tremendous leg strength. He breaks tackles and bowls people over. He's quick and he's fearless.

It was a promising end to the first half of the season. Our defense allowed the Saints only 232 yards, 71 on their final drive. I had six solo tackles and felt I played well. But the coaches were upset that our center Bart Oates and Simms muffed two more snaps to give them five muffs in five games.

"The thing about that fumble that really irked me," Oates said of his first botched play at the Saints' two, "is that we could have been on the way to annihilating these guys and because of my stupid snap, it's a [close] game." Oates' problem was that he was moving before completing the snap, causing the ball to evade Simms' hands. "I have it isolated," Oates said. "I don't have it licked. I've got to practice it so it's instinct."

A year ago, we were 4–4 at mid-season and finished 9–7. Now

we were 5–3, one game behind Dallas in our division. And we felt we had a better team. John Madden said about us, "Their offensive line has been one of their problems for years but now they're playing well. They've got a little running game going now. Their offense is so much better when they run."

Parcells and general manager George Young built the line: five big, strong, smart, white guys. Parcells nicknamed them "The Suburban Offensive Line" because he said their names sounded like a law firm: Benson, Ard, Oates, Godfrey & Nelson.

"We're the type of guys mom used to drive to practice," Oates said.

"We're all have roughly the same socioeconomic status," Benson said.

Brad Benson, the left tackle, is supposed to be too small for tackle at 6'3" and 270 pounds. But he has been a Giant since 1977, when we signed him as a free agent. First Jeff Weston was going to replace him; Weston developed knee trouble and retired. Then we drafted William Roberts in the first round in 1984. Roberts started the first eight games at left tackle as a rookie, with Benson moving to right guard. But Roberts suffered a foot injury, Benson moved back to left tackle, and Chris Godfrey moved in at right guard. In 1985, Benson finally was supposed to become a backup swingman, but Roberts suffered a major knee injury in camp. Parcells put Benson back at left tackle for his seventh season as a starter. A lot of players talk only about the next woman they're going to screw. Brad's always talking about his wife, his carpet, his dogs, his snowmobile. He's worked in the off-season at a bank in Secaucus. He's straighter than I am.

Brad's upset that he's entering his tenth season and still doesn't have a bubble gum card. The ultimate in pro sports isn't making an all-star team; it's having your own bubble gum card. As a kid, you collect cards. I did. It took me three or four years to get mine. Then it struck me: somewhere out there, kids are collecting *my* card.

Left guard Bill Ard, a stockbroker in the off-season, has been a starter since late in his rookie year, 1981. He looks so squeaky clean that I once told him to let his beard grow and not to brush his teeth. You have to be mean to play this game. Ard's father, Bill Sr., has been a Giants' season-ticket holder for more than 20 years. Billy went to Watchung (N.J.) High School. At the draft in 1981, some of his family had a banner that said, LET ARD BE YOUR GUARD. They were ecstatic when we chose him in the eighth round out of Wake Forest.

Bill's becoming a Giant fulfilled his father's dreams. I knew Billy could play in this league the first time we played Dallas and he wasn't awed by facing Randy White. He held his own. He may look like an altar boy, but he's tough.

"I remember seeing Gale Sayers and Dick Butkus play the Giants in Yankee Stadium with my father," Ard said. "He took me to games a couple of times a year. We sat in the end zone bleachers. I loved the atmosphere. But when I was young, I always wanted to be a baseball player. Midway through high school, I quit baseball to concentrate on football. . . . I always wanted to play for the Giants."

Center Oates came to us from the USFL during training camp in 1985. He is a Brigham Young University graduate and a Mormon. He's a serious guy, and fits right in. Uses power and finesse. We needed a replacement for the injured Kevin Belcher, and Oates stepped in. Benson kids him by saying, "Say hello to your two wives for me."

Bart was born in Mesa, Arizona. He is 6'3", weighs 265, and is a two-time Academic All-American. He spent three years with the USFL's Philadelphia Stars, starting 52 games over that span. He's kind of quiet, a good family man. But going into the playoffs, he got real vocal. He never turned down an interview. He seemed to revel in the attention.

The right guard, Chris Godfrey, 6'3", 265, is our team philosopher. He has an opinion about everything. He also is a USFL-jumper. He had played with the Michigan Panthers. It took a while until injuries made a place for him, but ever since he made the lineup he's stayed there. Chris looks like a choirboy, but looks are deceiving. He will knock your butt in the dirt if he gets the chance. Another quiet, all-American boy type. But I bet when he was a kid they said, "Don't bother him. He's dangerous."

Right tackle Karl Nelson, who is 6'6", 285, works as an engineer in the off-season. He's another strong, silent type. Nelson is an Iowa State man who spent the whole 1983 season on the injured reserve list, worked hard to learn the offense, and started every game for us in 1984 and 1985. An injury to Gordon King, who broke an arm late in the 1983 season, created a spot for Nelson. King never has been able to regain his starting job. Nelson has a large trunk, which helps him get good leverage. He's learned a lot from Benson.

After the Saints' game, we had to leave as quickly as we could because Hurricane Juan was approaching. The scariest part was taking off. It was windy, and it seemed to take an eternity for us to lift off the runway. We all remembered that a few years ago a plane crashed near here due to a wind shear.

Marshall and McGriff stayed in Louisiana because we had Monday and Tuesday off. Parcells gives us an extra day off after victories. It's great to get away from football, especially in the second half of the season. After a win, we usually start chanting, ''Two days off!'' But this time, it wasn't necessary. He just said he'd see us Wednesday, which got a big cheer.

The flight back was typical. Guys do various things. Mostly, they try to relax. Assistant coaches Len Fontes and Lamar Leachman got into a poker game with Lawrence Taylor, Phil Simms, and Andy Headen. There were other games going on, too. Some guys read. Godfrey and Nelson were reading best-sellers. Kenny Hill was writing letters. Some guys were reading the bible with George Martin.

Sometimes, Lawrence and I will mimic the flight attendants while they tell you how to fasten seatbelts and put the mask over your face. Sometimes, we'll pass out food and collect trays. We weren't fooling around this time, though. We were just trying to beat out the hurricane. It was pretty serious.

12 Background

I AM THE YOUNGEST of six children born to Edgar and Gladys Carson in Florence, South Carolina, in the northeastern corner of the state. I have two brothers, Douglas and Edgar, and three sisters, Louise, Ruth, and Loretta.

I had a good childhood. There was a lot of love and respect in our home. We went to church every Sunday. I used to make bows and arrows and hunt play animals. I was a normal, black, middle lower-class child. I was inquisitive. One time I discovered my Christmas presents behind a bed. I unwrapped one and started playing with a cap gun. My sister made me put it back.

I'm told I was more than 10 pounds when I was born. My sister Ruth did a lot to help raise me. I was the baby in the family and I had a great racket. I talked when I felt like talking. Otherwise I just pointed to things I wanted. My sister Loretta was my interpreter. I started talking for good when I was 3. I remember fixing my own bottle. Maybe I was a little spoiled. If I ever needed anything, my sisters did their best to get it for me. That's the way my whole family was.

My father was a career railroad man from Macon, Georgia, who came to South Carolina while working on the railroad and met my mother. I don't know exactly what he did. I think he fixed trains, but I know he was a heavy drinker and a soft touch. He was one of those guys who would work all week and then lose half his check before he came home—either on booze or lending it to somebody. The lights in our house used to go off once in a while. I thought it was a power outage. Then I'd find out my father hadn't paid the electric bill.

I saw him falling-down drunk only once. But I think he went out for a few drinks every night. You could smell it on him. He used to drink moonshine whiskey sometimes. Even though he was the way he was, we all respected him. But my dad wasn't really the best dad. There were times he put other people before us. I remember times when my sisters had to go without because he took money that he was supposed to give to them for their prom. I think he sometimes let his friends take advantage of him.

He was a very small man, like 5'5" and 135 pounds. He used to carry a gun. Why, I don't know. My brothers take after him, physically. I'm the only one who grew up big. I can remember going with my mother when I was real young to take my father his lunch. Later in his life he owned a bar for a couple of years, then drove a taxi. I loved him.

When I was five, there was a lady named Ida who lived down the street who got me to run numbers for her. She would send me to people's houses with a piece of paper and a dollar and I'd deliver them. I really didn't know what was going on. But when I came back, I got a nickel or some chewing gum. Numbers in the black community are a way of life. People have it hard, and so they dream. Some play numbers in their dreams.

When I was six, I'd sit on my steps and watch people go to work in the morning. That was my big excitement. I had a grand aunt who worked in the laundry room at a hospital. It was always a thrill to meet her at the bus stop. She'd bring me home an apple or some other present.

When I was very young, I remember the Ku Klux Klan marched through town. I was with my parents and didn't know what was going on. I saw guys walking down the streets in white robes and hoods in broad daylight. There was no reaction, really. It was just something that was more or less accepted down there. It was a spectacle, like the circus. To a child, it was just a march. They weren't bothering anyone. As I got older, I realized what the Klan represented. Then my attitude was that it was OK, as long as they didn't bother me.

I can remember going into department stores in the South and using a water fountain labeled for BLACKS ONLY. I remember going to a doctor's office and using the blacks' entrance. I just accepted it. I was young and didn't know any better.

I used to hide in the back seat of my father's car so he'd have to take me with him. Sometimes, he'd go visit a woman who wasn't my mother. Then a few days later, I'd be out with my mother and father. We'd pass the same house and I'd blurt out, "Daddy went here the other day and went in *that* house." I guess I got him in trouble a few times.

One time I borrowed my father's favorite rod and reel, bought a license, and went fishing in a creek. While I was fishing, the handle fell off the reel and got lost in the water. I came home and put it back in my father's drawer without the handle. Then he came home, saw what happened, and came into my room. I made believe I was sleeping. He took the rod and started hitting me with it. I just hid under the covers. He really wasn't hurting me.

I used to watch the *CBS Evening News* with Douglas Edwards. This was before Walter Cronkite. I remember thinking during the Cuban missile crisis that I should go out and dig a fallout shelter. I used to watch soap operas every day, like *The Edge of Night*, *As the World Turns* and *The Secret Storm*. In 1979, I appeared on an episode of *One Life to Live* as Frank (Big Bird) Sparrow, a player for the mythical Cougars football team.

I got my start in football with the Boys' Club. The club was in a part of Florence called The Block, where all the black people hung out. It was about 10 blocks from my house. We lived in a row of wooden houses with fences and yards. The Block was more like the city. There were pool halls, bars, social clubs, after-hours joints. It was a place where white people usually didn't go. Chances were there'd be a fight on Friday or Saturday night and somebody would get shot. Anyway, that's where the Boys' Club was. My team was all black.

My mother was a domestic. She worked as a cook at a country club and brought home leftover food. Cakes and things. When my dad got laid off from his job with the railroad, she figured the best thing for her to do was leave. There weren't a lot of job opportunities in South Carolina.

She went to Newark, New Jersey. I was about 6. I know it was one of the toughest things she had to do in her life. She loved us but she had to leave for a better job. She sent money home. She explained it all to me, and I understood. Women didn't leave their husbands back then. It was "til death do us part." I was very close to my mother. She taught me to be independent.

My mom worked in Newark for about 15 years. She would come home for holidays like Christmas and Easter and for our birthdays and graduations. But my sisters raised me. They did a pretty good job.

My mother told me she wasn't always going to be there so I had to learn to take care of myself. I learned how to cook by watching my mother. I can clean, wash, iron, and sew. I can do anything a woman can do, except have babies.

Just before my mother left, our house was destroyed by fire. I think it was in 1960. Everything we had went up in flames. I was burned. So was my brother, Douglas. It was late one Friday night. The fire was caused by an oil leak in the stove.

I remember waking up and I could see only red. A fireman woke me up and threw me out the window to another fireman. I woke up the next morning at a relative's house, wanting to watch television. *Mighty Mouse* was my favorite show. I didn't realize my brother was in serious condition in the hospital. We stayed at friends' houses for a while until we got relocated. We didn't have any insurance, so we just had to start over from scratch. I think that might be why I don't try to hold onto anything so tightly as an adult. I realize it can be taken from me at any time. My family never owned a house. We just rented.

I joined the Boy Scouts at about age ten. I loved scouting. I learned leadership and independence. I could start a fire, administer first aid, find my way in the woods. One time I went to a camp and took up smoking. Then we were going for swimming merit badges and we had to swim across a lake. I only made it halfway, then my wind gave out. A boat picked me up. That's when I gave up smoking.

One reason I started playing football was that in eighth grade I went to a Wilson High game on a Friday night and saw that, after the game, the girls would flock around the players. I said to myself, I've got to get into this. Wilson was the black high school in Florence, back before desegregation.

The next year, I went out for the football team as a freshman. The other guys were a lot bigger than me. That didn't bother me, though —the training did. After one or two days of practice, I quit. I couldn't take it. One night after practice, my sister told me I was doing pushups in my sleep in bed. I got involved with the Boys' Club team because that was more fun. They didn't train so hard.

In tenth grade I had a growth spurt up to about 190 pounds. I went out for the Wilson High varsity and made the team as a defensive lineman. I didn't play too much. The next year desegregation came. I had the option of staying at Wilson or transferring to the school closer to home—McClenaghan.

Most of my friends decided to go to McClenaghan, which became integrated, so I did, too. I made the football team as a junior and also got involved in ROTC. I was always fascinated with the military. I admired soldiers when they came home in their pressed uniforms and shiny shoes. Back then soldiers came home on leave and they wore their uniforms to the grocery store. That was pre-Vietnam.

I've always had a fascination with planes. I enjoyed ROTC. I liked to drill and march and take orders and give orders. I learned all about different aircraft. At one point, I could tell you anything you'd want to know about every bomber, fighter plane, or spy plane we had. My favorite was the F-4 Phantom because it was so sleek.

As a group my ROTC unit visited Shaw Air Force Base in Sumter, about 40 miles from Florence. We also visited Myrtle Beach AFB. I was in awe just being around the military. It was a feeling I never really grew out of. My two brothers joined the Air Force. One left the military and became a minister. I think I would have joined if I had not been drafted by the Giants.

I started out my high school career as a 215-pound blocking back but eventually got switched to defense. At the end of my junior year, I was nominated for class president in a school that was about 60-40 white. There were two white candidates and they split the vote. All the blacks wound up voting for me. So I was elected. Eventually, I was promoted in ROTC to the rank of lieutenant colonel. I became a football star, too. My senior year began as a very enjoyable time. Until near the end of the season.

The team was coming back on a bus from a 0–0 tie. All the blacks were in the back, joking around. Some white guys in the front shouted back for us to shut up and made some remarks. The coach came back and told us to shut up. The following Monday, all the black players didn't show up for practice. They came to my house. After that, coach Ladson Cubbage thought I was the ringleader. Two weeks later, I sprained both my ankles in a game and missed the next one. Then, during the week, we were running sprints and the coach said, "Carson, if you can't run any faster than that, get off the field." So I quit the team with two games left in the season.

I considered that harassment racist. One of the reasons I chose all-black South Carolina State as my college was that I just wanted to get an education, have fun playing football and not have to worry about racism. I had been all set to go to North Carolina A&T, where I first met Willie Jeffries, an assistant coach there. But I got a letter telling me they didn't have the funds to offer me a scholarship. I had gone through high school neglecting my studies. I had nobody to push me. I heard from different colleges—Georgia, Tennessee, Colorado State —but they wanted me to go to a junior college first because of my grades.

One of my high school teachers, Dorothy McDuffie, took me to

S.C. State, her alma mater. State offered me a scholarship, so I went there. I wanted to be among people who understood me. I also was following a woman named Donna Hawkins, my girlfriend at the time. And I was only 90 minutes from home. I majored in health and physical education.

Jeffries, who had worked for Johnny Majors at Pittsburgh, got the S.C. State job before my sophomore year.

After they had gotten to know me, some female classmates told me they had been afraid to approach me because I always looked like I was mad. That helped me on the football field. I liked the fact that my looks were intimidating. Nobody messed with me on the field.

I gravitated naturally to a leadership role. Most of the players looked up to me and respected me. I was sort of pushed into it. I played hard and well. I didn't smoke, drink, or touch drugs. At times, I felt like a real square. But I always the type of person to be there when somebody needed me. I cared about players as human beings, but I couldn't get too close to anybody. I'm not sure why. But I've always felt that if you put your heart and soul into something and get rejected, it's devastating.

I never went to house parties because I knew there would be smoking dope and alcohol there and I didn't want to get into that. I felt fortunate to be in college on a scholarship. I knew if I kept my nose clean and stayed out of trouble, I'd get a free education. I looked at myself as a student athlete and took a lot of pride in that.

Being in college was the first time I ever was away from home. In my first semester, I was one-tenth of a point away from being placed on academic probation. It was a result of laziness and not being accustomed to the college routine of combining studies and football.

My freshman year, the pro scouts were coming to see my teammate, Barney Chavous, and Bobby Beathard, then of the Miami Dolphins, told me he was impressed with me and thought I might be able to play pro ball some day. That inspired me.

Looking back on it, I would have paid to play at South Carolina State. It was one of the happiest and most fulfilling periods of my life. I had grown up admiring guys like Bubba Smith, Willie Davis, Buck Buchanan, and Deacon Jones, who went to S.C. State. I used to watch NFL games every Sunday as a teenager. After games, I'd get an old T-shirt, grab a marker and write my favorite player's name on the back. I was a down lineman in those days, so I idolized them. But I didn't root for any one pro team.

Deacon Jones and I wore the same number, 75. State retired my number in 1978 between halves of a game they played at Giants Stadium, a 27–0 victory over Howard. One time Deacon and I were at a reception in Hawaii at the governor's mansion during Pro Bowl week. He told me I must have paid somebody off because they wouldn't retire the number after *he* had worn it.

At the football banquet after my senior year, I made a speech after being chosen the best all-around athlete at State for the second straight year. I said I wish I could have played four more years. The fans down there really cared about you. So did the teachers and the coaches. You weren't just a piece of meat.

You didn't see any illegal payments to players or anybody cutting corners. It was a classy school and a classy program. Nobody got any no-show jobs, like turning sprinklers on and off for $12 an hour. That's what some of my Giants' teammates told me they did at an Atlantic Coast Conference school.

There was nothing like a football game in Orangeburg, S.C., on a Saturday afternoon or night. Our colors were garnet and blue. You walked to the stadium and the students wished you good luck. Nobody cared about the point spread. We just knew we were going to win. During football season, there was a sense of pride throughout the whole school and the city. It was like an electric current.

We played on a field that was better maintained than most NFL fields. Everybody had pride. The groundskeepers, the fans, the band. The band was called The Marching 101. They practiced just as hard as we did. And they played the national anthem better than I'd ever heard it played. Sometimes when I'm standing on the field next to coach Parcells at a Giant game and the band's playing, I don't hear it. I hear The Marching 101.

Jeffries made all his players run 12 minutes on Sunday mornings after every game. We all had to run at least seven laps—a mile and three quarters. He would stand there as each player came off the track. If you had alcohol in your system, he could smell it in your sweat. If he did, there'd be disciplinary action. He didn't want us to smoke or chew, either. And he didn't like facial hair. Nobody challenged him. Some coaches are fat and sloppy. Not Jeff. He used to work out with us. And he cared about each player like a son.

I never missed a college game in four years. I was MVP in our conference my last two seasons and an Associated Press Little All-America my senior year, when I received an award for having the highest academic average among black college all-stars. Not bad for a guy who used to schedule his classes so as not to conflict with *The Young and the Restless*.

We had a strong defense. My senior year I think we only gave up 29 points. We sometimes held the other team under 100 total yards for a game. I had 114 unassisted tackles, 41 assists, and 30 quarterback sacks. Thirty! My coaches started telling me I'd make it in the NFL. Coming from a small school, I wanted to prove I could compete with guys from football factories like Notre Dame, USC, and Ohio State.

But I wouldn't trade my time at S.C. State for a full ride anywhere else. On Saturday nights, we had various groups come in and play like Earth, Wind and Fire and Kool and the Gang. The football team was a rallying point for campus life. I ended up being on the Dean's List, a two-year football team captain, and president of the student union in my senior year. I got my degree in four years. I think about 40 percent of our team went through college in four years. Many of the guys who did not graduate on time were in that predicament because they changed majors, and a good percentage of them graduated after years.

At S.C. State, we practiced twice a day five times during the week. On those days you had to be up at five to be on the field at six. Then you had breakfast. Then we had another practice after classes in the afternoon and team meetings at night. It was a good preparation for the pros.

Jeffries and I were friends, on and off the field. I could always talk to him about any problems or feelings I had. When I came home, after another losing season with the Giants, I always told him pro football wasn't like it was when I was a Bulldog.

"We only lost three or four games when Harry was there," Jeffries said. "He always liked discipline and organization. That's why he was such a great leader. At bed check, we didn't have to worry about no noise after the coaches left."

One night we were staying at a hotel and some girls came over. I ran them all away. I didn't want any of the guys getting in trouble. I didn't want to read about them in the paper the next day.

I had a great relationship with Jeffries. I remember one day I really didn't want to practice. I told him, "Coach, I could tell you I have diarrhea or a groin pull or something to get out of practice, but the plain truth is that I just don't feel like practicing today." He looked at me, told me he understood, and that I should go up to the dorm and stay there. That's the kind of relationship we had.

My father died of a stroke the summer before my senior year. Coach Jeffries broke the news. I think one or two tears fell, but I was pretty composed. I knew he was dying so it really wasn't a big shock. My mother died in 1979, so I became sort of a patriarch for my sisters. Two of them live in a house I bought them in Florence. One's single, the other's divorced with two children. They helped me growing up, so I decided to help them.

I made the transition to pro football pretty easily. In my heart, I'm a defensive lineman. There are times I wish I could alternate between the line and linebacker. In my senior year, they switched me to middle guard so teams couldn't run away from me. Middle guard wasn't a whole lot different from middle linebacker. You read the center and react.

My first pro contract included a $20,000 signing bonus and salaries of $32,500, $37,000, and $42,500. When I first came up, I'd have played for free. I loved the game that much. I still love it. But there comes a time when all players realize pro football is a business. You have to separate that aspect of it from the game itself. I think I've been able to do that.

13

Game No. 9

Giants 22
Tampa Bay 20

A Fuzzy Feeling

THE DAY AFTER the New Orleans game, the Giants took a calculated risk and waived kicker Jess Atkinson, even though he had made 10 of 15 field goal tries. The deadline for activating Mark Haynes had arrived, so somebody had to go to create a roster opening. It was another business decision.

Parcells did not know if Ali Haji-Sheikh was ready. He intended to watch Haji-Sheikh kick in practice. Ali is loose, articulate, and well-liked by teammates. He works hard. He does not rattle in the clutch. But a kicker can't kick with a sore leg. Parcells' patience with him was wearing thin. The Giants had hoped Atkinson would go unclaimed so if Haji-Sheikh was not ready, the Giants could re-sign Atkinson just before our next game and release somebody else. But that plan was foiled. St. Louis claimed Atkinson on waivers, releasing Neil O'Donoghue.

So Parcells brought in Eric Schubert, a rookie from Pittsburgh who had a tryout with us in camp. Schubert was working as a substitute teacher and part-time assistant coach at Lakeland Regional High School in Wanaque, N.J. To make room for Schubert, the Giants placed rookie defensive back Tyrone Davis on the IR list. I had to laugh at that.

Davis had played on special teams in New Orleans and looked fine. The team said Davis had recurring back spasms which would take at least four weeks to heal. I didn't understand why they just didn't IR

Davis Monday when they activated Haynes. Then they could have kept Atkinson. He had made seven field goals in a row before his two misses in New Orleans. But then I'm not the general manager.

"It's good to get a job back," Schubert said on arrival. "The only problem is, I need tickets [for friends]. I need about a hundred."

"Hey, Schubert," hollered our defensive line coach Lamar Leachman, "Enjoy it. The last guy who had your locker is gone."

Leachman reminds us of that cartoon character, Foghorn Leghorn. He has a blustery voice but a heart of gold. And boy does he make practices interesting by bellowing and cajoling. When Lamar, now 52, was hired by Ray Perkins in 1980 to take Jim Stanley's place, he was our seventh defensive line coach in eight seasons. I had no idea Lamar would end the turmoil.

Leachman was a center and linebacker at Tennessee and had been a college assistant coach at four places. Before coming to the Giants, he was defensive line coach of the New York Stars in the defunct World Football League and served five years with two teams in the Canadian Football League.

Leachman is big on inspirational signs in his office. One of them is IT'S NOT THE PIGMENT OF A MAN'S SKIN WHICH TELLS HIM IF HE WILL SUCCEED OR FAIL, BUT WHAT'S IN HIS HEART. Another is AS LONG AS YOU'RE GREEN, YOU CONTINUE TO GROW. IT'S WHEN YOU THINK YOU'RE RIPE, YOU'RE ROTTEN.

"I use the signs more or less as a motivational factor," Leachman said. "I would hope that they would help us play with a little more enthusiasm, a little more intensity."

Everybody on our team impersonates Lamar. The best was Floyd Eddings, a little receiver no longer with the team. He used to do his thing on planes coming home from games. He put rolled up T-shirts under his shirtsleeves, because Lamar has huge biceps and triceps. Lamar has a way of getting on guys in practice but still making it fun. He loves to teach. He loves us. After each game we win, he comes around and kisses guys on the forehead. If somebody gets a fumble or an interception during a game, Lamar will kiss their helmets. Of course, he can get on your nerves, too, because he just never lets up. I know sometimes he gets Jim Burt so mad he'd like to boot him in the behind.

Meanwhile, management resumed negotiations with our last remaining holdout, wide receiver Earnest Gray. Earnie had taken a calculated risk and lost. He played out his option in 1984. Naturally, nobody tried to sign him as a free agent. Free agency in the NFL is a farce. It doesn't work because the compensation formula is weighted against player movement.

Gray, 28, was our No. 6 receiver in club history with 243 catches in six seasons. Our fans seemed to remember his drops more than his catches. But Gray tied for the NFC lead in 1983 with 78 receptions. Let's face it, though. He wasn't as consistent as James Lofton and he wasn't a game-breaker. He was a possession receiver. Short and medium-range stuff. He'd go over the middle but rarely beat people deep.

A fractured hand limited Gray to seven catches in our last eight games, including the playoffs, in 1984. Then he priced himself off the team. Management felt it could win without him, since rookies Bobby Johnson and Lionel Manuel had good years. Gray turned down a Giants' contract offer of $900,000 for three years. He got bad advice from his agent, Bob McDonald, who claimed he was dickering with the USFL's Memphis Showboats. Gray was seeking $1.2 million for three years. But since the USFL was falling apart, he had no leverage. He brooded at home in Memphis with his wife and daughter. We hope a better system of free agency is included in our next collective bargaining agreement after the old one expires in 1987.

But I was not worried about Gray the week before our Tampa game. I was watching film of Buccaneers' running back James Wilder. Tampa Bay was 0–8 but Wilder had rushed for 735 of his team's 790 yards and had caught 36 passes. I knew we were going to have to stop him in order to beat the Bucs. I knew it would not be easy. Our plan was to attack Wilder from a ''lane'' defense in which we'd hold our ground and not give him any holes.

Our track record is that we let down against easier teams. We lost games to the Bucs in 1979 and 1980 in Tampa and beat them by only 17–14 at Giants Stadium in 1984, when Wilder rushed for 112 yards and caught 65 yards worth of passes. After the game, Lawrence Taylor said of Wilder, ''He is the best back I ever played against in my life.''

Wilder is an outstanding athlete. He works hard. He's a very humble guy. I met him at the Pro Bowl after the 1984 season. He's not the fastest back in the league, but he's one of the toughest. And he's an excellent pass receiver coming out of the backfield. The Bucs use him as a lone setback in a formation with two tight ends. I have to guess which way he's going.

Our left linebacker Byron Hunt said of Wilder, ''He's an open, wilder type of runner. I guess the name fits him. He runs with a lot of aggressiveness and that makes it harder to tackle him.'' Hunt suffered a hyperextended elbow trying to tackle Wilder in a 1984 game.

"My style is a combination of speed, strength, and maneuvering,'' Wilder said. "I'd say I try to read the defense and go in the opposite direction.''

"He's the most bruising runner I've been around,'' Bucs' guard Steve Courson, who has blocked for Franco Harris, said. "He's a slashing runner who goes north-south, never east-west. You know he'll hit the hole hard. There won't be any monkeying around.''

Despite Wilder's overwhelming presence, we could not forget about their tight end, Jimmie Giles. He had caught four touchdown passes against Miami the week before and was playing like an all-pro again after several down years.

The Bucs used Jerry Bell as a second tight end. Bell was the motion guy, meaning he was mostly a blocking decoy. He'd get up a head of steam running laterally across the formation and then turn up—just like Washington's wham play. So we prepared for that.

The Bucs also liked to run a Washington-type counter play and also would fake the counter and throw play-action passes to the tight end coming across the middle. So our preparation for Tampa Bay was much the same as it was for the Redskins. We knew that Bucs' quarterback Steve DeBerg had come from San Francisco, where he was a product of the Bill Walsh system of short passes to set up runs. DeBerg did not throw deep often. But he would throw it in the seats rather than accept a sack. He has a very quick release. but I don't think he reads defenses very well. I got an interception against him in 1984.

It's always a thrill to get an interception. I had told my daughter before that game that I was going to get one for her—and I did. That really made me feel great, when they put the camera on me and I said, "Aja, this one's for you.''

We knew the Bucs' defense was allowing 31 points a game and wasn't playing as well as usual. They missed defensive end Lee Roy Selmon, out for the year with a back problem which eventually would force his retirement, and Hugh Green, an impact linebacker who was traded to Miami after questioning the Bucs' defensive scheme. You had to feel great for Green. He went from a winless team to a Super Bowl contender. I wish it was that easy. But I'm resigned to the fact that the Giants probably never will trade me.

The week before the Tampa Bay game, clubhouse man Vinnie Swerc told a reporter he had cleaned out Lawrence Taylor's locker by throwing out several years of unopened fan mail. Some of them said like, "Hi, Lawrence. I've always been a fan of yours. My brother has so-and-so illness. Would you mind sending him an autographed photo to so-and-so hospital."

I always answer every piece of fan mail I get. Not always on time, but I always get to it. I know it can make a person's day. It can get kind of expensive, with the cost of photos and postage. And it takes time to read through the letters. But I always try to get a feel for the person and put the appropriate response on the photo. Then I have a lot of people who write back to me, thanking me for writing to them. That makes me feel good to know they're feeling good. But Lawrence is the kind of guy who always seems to be busy. He plays golf on his days off, listens to business propositions. He's really not into fans. Some other players are like that, too. They feel they're only there to play ball, not to be public relations men. They feel they don't want to compete in popularity contests.

On Tuesday before the Tampa Bay game, I spent most of the day cramming for my midterm examination in the management course I was taking once a week at Fairleigh Dickinson University. (I got an 87 and a B-plus in the course.) I hope to get a master's degree in business some day, although I don't know exactly what I want to do after I retire as a player.

The Giants' organization cares about its players more than most teams in the NFL. This stems from the top. The Maras are family men and Wellington, especially, has sought to cultivate a family atmosphere in the team. Whenever a player leaves the Giants, he'll never say anything against the Maras. The coaches and George Young, maybe. But not the owners. The team arranged through a consultant, Joel Goldberg, to have players take courses at FDU with a view toward their post-football lives. Sixteen signed up. The other fifteen were taking undergraduate courses. I was working on my MBA. Going to class was like a breath of fresh air to me, a chance to get away from football once a week.

Nobody in my class knew who I was until a television station came over and shot footage in the classroom. Nobody bothered me. The rest of the students came to class after work just like I did. They didn't want to go out for a beer or anything. A few students came up to me and asked some questions about football, but I didn't really get the celebrity treatment.

Anyway, the day after my midterm at FDU, I got my midterm grades from the defensive coordinator, Bill Belichick. He told me I was the Giant's most consistent defensive player and thanked me for the leadership I'd provided. He told me I was playing better than I had in

1984. But players don't pay much attention to all these computer print-outs and grades the coaches work up. We know who's playing well and who isn't.

Belichick is only a year older than I am. He started in the NFL in 1975 as a $1,300-a-year assistant with the Baltimore Colts. Ray Perkins hired him as a special teams' coach in 1979. When Perkins left after the 1982 season and Parcells was promoted, he retained Belichick, later promoting him to defensive coordinator.

Belichick knows football. But his studious nature makes him the butt of jokes and his voice puts people to sleep. Casey Merrill wrote "Captain Sominex" on the blackboard before one of our team meetings in 1985. Taylor said he would like to take Belichick home—to help Taylor's wife Linda get his two kids to fall asleep.

Casey always sits with his chair against the wall and it's very obvious when he's sleeping. But whenever Belichick would ask him a question, invariably Casey knew the answer. Belichick could never catch Casey sleeping. One time, Casey hit his elbow into the wall five times trying to keep himself awake. Bill didn't appreciate that.

Anyway, my football grade notwithstanding, I still was upset that I had been getting cut-blocked below the knees by offensive linemen. I had been looking at the ballcarrier instead of the linemen. Blocks below the knees can be devastating on misdirection plays, where you're focused one way and you get hit from the side. Sometimes you get popped right in the facemask with the other guy's helmet and it rattles your brain a little.

On Thursday, I took a night off from watching film and went trick-or-treating with my daughter. Parcells let me out of practice early. I just kept my entire uniform on, putting black under my eyes. I got a Raggedy Ann costume for Aja. She didn't like it. She wanted to be a princess, but I couldn't find a princess costume. Aja and I went from house to house by car in my neighbood in Ossining. We went only to neighbors I knew, about 15 houses altogether. Aja got a great assortment of candy. The neighbors were really surprised to see me, but we all enjoyed it. Aja wanted to get back early so she could watch the Cosby show.

Three days later, I woke up at 4 a.m. before our Tampa Bay game. I had taken a sleeping pill the night before but it hadn't worked. I was restless and upset because I started thinking that I was underpaid. I had approached Young in 1984 about renegotiating my contract and he redid the incentive clauses. But I was still upset. The incentives go in the face of team play. And that bothered me. It made me more conscious of the incentives instead of just playing. My contract said that I'd get

$15,000 if I led the team in tackles and $10,000 for finishing second. The Giants upped my Pro Bowl incentive from $10,000 to $20,000. If I played more than 70 percent of the plays with the defense, I would get another $10,000 (I wound up doing so.) But subconsciously, I was upset.

Here I was in my 10th season, after making six Pro Bowls, with a base salary of $300,000. Taylor, with four Pro Bowls in four years, was making $750,000, making him the highest paid linebacker in the NFL. The Giants had told me I was too valuable to trade, but they wouldn't redo my contract. And yet they did redo Perry Williams' contract. Perry told me about it one day at practice. So nothing is written in stone.

I wasn't the only one in an inequitable situation. Brad Benson, in his seventh year as a starter, was making $175,000. Conrad Goode, a second-year reserve, got a contract for more than $1 million when he signed in 1984. And Carl Banks—he was the second player chosen in the 1984 draft and is getting $2.6 million over four years. I like Carl as a person, but if he disappeared, we wouldn't miss him.

I like George Martin, too. But he's a former No. 11 draft pick. He's never made a Pro Bowl. And he made $325,000 in 1985—$25,000 more than me. It's too bad that the only alternative I have is to sit out. I made a mistake signing a long-term contract in 1983. I wanted the security. I got a good contract at the time. I was right up there with Randy Gradishar and Jack Lambert. But a bidding war with the USFL sent NFL salaries skyrocketing in 1983–1984, and I was locked in. Fourteen linebackers in the NFL had higher base salaries than I did in 1985, including guys like the Raiders' Rod Martin, the 49ers' Keena Turner, Denver's Tom Jackson, and two Green Bay linebackers, John Anderson and Mike Douglass.

In April 1986, the Giants were negotiating with USFL offensive tackle Gary Zimmerman, who is 6'6", 270 pounds and would have been more insurance for us. It was reported that the Giants offered Zimmerman a four-year, $1.4 million contract which would pay him $650,000 in salary and bonuses in 1986. And he never had played in an NFL game! But Zimmerman balked at playing on the East Coast and the Giants traded him to Minnesota for two second-round 1986 draft picks. So you can understand why I felt ignored and cheated. In September, 1985, I'd asked George Young about trying to find an arbitrator to mediate the Mark Haynes dispute. Young said he would refuse to abide by an arbitrator's decision. I also told George I was upset with my own situation. He claimed his hands were tied. By who, he wouldn't say. The Maras, I guess. I sent Young some vaseline after the Washington game and told him, "When you fuck me, it hurts." I know it was crude, but I was really upset.

I thought about taking a hike for a few days, but I felt that it would not have gone over too well with management or the public. The public thinks I'm flaky, partly because I project that image but also because the Giants have. My teammates and some reporters know better. Common sense dictates there is no logical reason why I should earn less than half of Taylor's salary. But that's the way it was. My only option was to withhold my services—which I wasn't going to do.

My contract provided for deferred money. I think a lot of players make a big mistake taking all the cash up front. They live in the fast lane and wind up blowing most of their money on bad investments, cars, houses, and other things. For tax reasons I wanted to spread my salary over a longer period.

One hundred thousand dollars of my 1983 and 1984 salaries of $250,000 and $275,000 were deferred. I deferred $125,000 of my $300,000 salary in 1985 and will defer $150,000 of my $350,000 salary for 1986.

Deferring the money puts me in a lower tax bracket. But if I want the money, I can start getting it on April 1 of the first year after I retire. I'll also be eligible for $120,000 in severance pay from the Giants when I leave the game. My agent Craig Kelly and I were trying to convince the Giants to put my deferred money in an annuity, where at least it would accrue interest for me. But again, I don't have much leverage.

Anyway, I got over thinking about my contract and started thinking about Wilder. We were able to contain him this time, limiting him to 75 yards in 21 carries and two catches for 20 yards. But the Bucs gave us a tough game.

We got five field goals—of 24, 36, 24, 41, and 33 yards—from Schubert, who became an immediate celebrity, and another strong running game from Joe Morris (132 yards). The defense also played a good game. And we pulled into a first-place tie with Dallas, which was upset by St. Louis, in the NFC East. Our 6–3 record equaled our best start since 1970.

It was a day for small people—Morris (5'7"), Schubert (5'8") and Phil McConkey (5'10")—at Giants Stadium. McConkey set up our only touchdown with a 17-yard punt return and a 13-yard clutch catch. "The NFL should pay attention to this game," Casey Merrill said. "Size in the NFL is overrated. Too often, management and coaches make a mistake looking at the numbers—height, weight, speed in the 40-yard dash. I've seen more No. 1 picks who are washouts and more free agents make it than you'd believe. You can't measure the heart of Morris and the tenacity of Schubert."

"Size doesn't matter," Schubert said. "Heart does."

Schubert had been making $36 a day teaching, plus the $1,000 he was to receive as assistant football coach at his alma mater. He received $3,125 for playing against Tampa, one-sixteenth of the $50,000 NFL minimum salary. "I guess it will sink in tonight," he said of his accomplishment, "when I see it on the news."

In the classroom, Schubert taught math, science, metal shop, Latin, and French. "I baby-sat, really," he said. "The teacher leaves a lesson plan. You just go over it, make sure no one causes trouble or tries to leave."

His five field goals were one shy of our team record. Each kick was necessary, since our offense sputtered all day. "Before the last one," Schubert said, "Jim Burt told me, 'We need one more. If you kick this one, we're going to win it.'"

"Look at you," Parcells said to Schubert after the television lights had been doused, "you're a star now. You hit your own Lotto."

That was a private joke. Parcells had told Schubert on Wednesday that he did not know if Haji-Sheikh would be ready. The next night, when Parcells called to say the Giants wanted to sign Schubert, he was out buying a lottery ticket.

"I didn't come close," he said.

The game was a seesaw. It was 3–3 after the first period. Then Bucs quarterback DeBerg hit Giles with a 25-yard scoring pass. Giles beat Terry Kinard on the play. I thought the ball was out of his reach, but he adjusted to it and made a great catch. Schubert kicked another field goal with three minutes left in the half and we trailed, 10–6. Then Tampa Bay drove back down the field to a second-and-goal at our three. They tried a pitch to Wilder, running to his right. I saw the linemen going that way and came up to meet Wilder. I saw an opening, shot through it and got a clean lick on Wilder with my shoulder. His thigh caught me in the helmet. I got up slowly and wobbled back to the huddle. I called the defense for the next play. DeBerg threw a pass and it went incomplete. I looked up at the scoreboard to see what down it was, and I could feel myself going out. I grabbed the arm of an official, and that's the last thing I can remember. I guess it was another concussion. I blacked out. I remember getting up and walking off the field. Then I was put on a cart and trucked into the dressing room.

The Bucs went on to kick a field goal and led 13–6 at halftime. But holding them without a touchdown proved to be very important. I regrouped mentally. Dr. Russell Warren asked me a few questions, like my name and who we were playing. I was sitting on a table in his office. Parcells asked me if I was OK and I said, "Yeah."

We did not want to provide the Bucs with their first victory. In the second half, we scored on a three-yard run by Morris to cap a 47-yard drive and added three more Schubert field goals to go ahead, 22–13. The Morris touchdown was made possible by Maurice Carthon, our battering ram of a fullback. On third-and-one at the Bucs' three, Morris swung left on a play we call Slant 17. Cornerback John Holt moved up. Carthon upended him. Morris scored.

"I just tried to hit him as hard as I could," Carthon said. "Nothing else he could do but go to the turf. He weighs 175, I weigh 227."

I don't know how anybody could play 18 games in the spring with the Generals and 23 more in the fall in the same year. But Maurice did. And we were happy to have him. "I'm not saying I don't have aches in my shoulders and legs," he said. "It's a mental thing. If you think of all you did, everybody would be tired."

With 2:27 left in the game, DeBerg capped a 78-yard drive with a one-yard pass to Giles. Tampa Bay forced our offense to punt after three downs, and the Bucs got the ball back trailing by two, 22–20. They would have been on our 38-yard line with 33 seconds left if Bucs' left tackle Sean Farrell had not been called for holding Merrill on third-and-10. DeBerg was intercepted by Kinard on the next play.

"It was a lousy call," Farrell said.

It was nice to have it go for us. It clearly was a holding penalty on Farrell. He was holding Merrill. He hogtied him and took him down. Offensive linemen do a lot of holding and it's never called. Then when they do get penalized, they resent it.

I had a little headache during the second half, but I was fine. When St. Louis beat Dallas the next night, we found ourselves tied for first place at 6–3 with the Cowboys. I also was a little sore after the Tampa Bay game from running into Courson. I had known Steve a long time. In my senior year, I used to drive to the University of South Carolina because they had better weight facilities than State did. That's where I met Courson. I was in awe of him. He looked like a weightlifter. He was a No. 5 pick in 1977 and fit right in with the Pittsburgh Steelers, with whom he earned two Super Bowl rings.

I've played against Steve a half-dozen times. He's more or less a straight-line blocker. He just comes at you, hits you, and you feel it. To combat the Bucs' blocking schemes, we shifted our line around and ran a gap-type defense in which we lined up across from the gaps created by their offensive line. They couldn't just fire out in a straight line and block us. We made them do something they didn't like to do. We also did some slanting, where we exchanged hole responsibilities. That confused the Bucs' blockers.

Courson confessed to *Sports Illustrated* that he had used steroids to get stronger. Offensive linemen can take steroids and get away with it because they move only in a straight line. Steroids increase your muscle mass, cost you some agility. And they can have harmful side-effects. We had a couple of guys on our team use them a few years ago. Jeff Weston was one. He got big real fast. It was a combination of weight lifting and steroids. Ernie Hughes was another. They were two of the strongest guys I've ever seen.

Steroids are not outlawed, but I never would take them. A defensive player needs to be loose, fluid. Too many muscles would slow me down. I need to retain my agility.

14

Game No. 10
Giants 24
Los Angeles Rams 19

A Four-Game Winning Streak

THE DAY AFTER our victory over the Buccaneers, *Good Morning America* called Schubert, representatives of three New York television stations drove to his house for interviews, and one chauffeured him to Manhattan for a *Live at Five* news spot. Three of America's 10 largest newspapers telephoned. Schubert said he got 23 calls in all. *Sports Illustrated* chose him as its NFL offensive player of the week.

"I'll be in *Sports Illustrated*?" Schubert told *Newsday* reporter Peter King, sitting in the Lakeland High superintendent's office. "You're kidding. Holy God! Not bad for my first game, huh?" Only in America.

Meanwhile, we received word that Rams' quarterback Dieter Brock would not play against us at Giants Stadium in our next game because he had a kidney stone removed from his abdomen. He would be replaced by backup Jeff Kemp, who had not attempted a pass all season. We knew Kemp from last year and we knew he did not have much of an arm. The Rams' offense was built around the running of Eric Dickerson.

Before this game, the Giants signed Earnest Gray for a reported $100,000 for the balance of the season and $250,000 for 1986. Of course, nobody expected him to be a Giant for long. One of the team's options was to release Gray after his two-week roster exemption expired. We figured that's what would happen.

"Whatever the decision is," Gray said, "it won't be the end of the world. If they decide to release me, then I'll go on with my career somewhere else. . . . I think I'd do the same thing if I had it to do all over again. The risk was there when I didn't accept their terms, and it was a risk I decided to take.''

Although the Rams were 8–1 coming into our game, we weren't awed. We had beaten them 16-10 in the 1984 playoffs in Los Angeles by stopping Dickerson. He was still the key to their offense. And we felt we could stop him again. The Rams' offense is pretty basic. They were winning on defense, just like we were.

We were very relaxed the week before the game. Football was starting to be fun. There were more smiles and not as much intensity in practice as you would expect before an important game. Some writers noted in their midweek stories that Casey Merrill was not playing as much and not making as great a contribution to our pass rush in 1985 as he had in 1984. It took him a while to perfect his techniques after his holdout.

You just can't come in off the street and play pro football. Casey depends on speed rushes a lot, working to the outside of the left offensive tackle. He needed time to get his timing down and work on exploding off the ball. Plus, Leonard Marshall had improved his pass rush so much that Casey was being called upon less and less. Merrill played only when Marshall needed a break.

We knew we needed a big game from our defensive line because the Rams have one of the biggest, toughest, most experienced offensive lines in the NFL. They use two tight ends, calling one a U-back. Their blocking tight end David Hill, who must weight 260 pounds, is one of the best in the league. His teammates call him Thundering Blubber. He is not much of a receiving threat. Neither are their wideouts, who are fast but have bad hands. They are used mainly as decoys.

"This isn't going to be very fancy, either side," Parcells said. "Both teams will try to get field position by defense and try to play error-free on offense."

Fans love to see the ball in the air, but offensive linemen prefer to run the ball. When an offensive lineman is run-blocking, he is attacking, punishing his opponent. When he is pass-blocking, he is retreating, absorbing blows. In our losses to Dallas and Cincinnati, 90 percent of our net yardage came on passing. In our latest three victories, we had rushed for more yards than we had passed, 553 to 506.

"We're a balanced team," Simms said, adding that he thought Joe Morris was the key. "Everybody's happy when the running game's doing the job, because then you don't have to rely on the pass."

The day before the game, the Giants activated Carl Banks, who had been out four weeks with a knee injury, from IR and released special teams' player Larry Flowers, who was claimed on waivers by the Jets.

We all missed Larry, a smiling, happy-go-lucky guy who is a super tackler on punts and kickoffs and wins our "Ugliest Player" contest every year in training camp. Larry got the news on Friday before practice.

Another business decision. Larry called me after he was cut. He said Parcells told him he had a couple of other options—like cutting backup defensive end Dee Hardison or backup fullback Rob Carpenter, who had been phased out of the offense. But Parcells told Flowers he did not want to leave himself short at those positions. It was a numbers thing and Larry got caught up in the numbers. I knew we'd miss him. Flowers was one of the best special-team tacklers we've ever had.

I called Flowers the Billy Martin of the Yankees because he'd been released and re-signed several times in the past. But this time, he would not be coming back. The Jets were in dire need of defensive backs and depth on special teams. At least Flowers, like Dave Jennings, would still be playing in Giants Stadium.

Our win over the Rams showed all the characteristics a winning team has to have. We came back from a 13–0 deficit and overcame a host of mistakes to win this one. We had some help from the officials but these things even out. In the pregame warmups, Mark Haynes injured a hamstring muscle, which indicated to me that he had not stretched out properly. His 1985 season would be a total loss.

On our first play from scrimmage, starting from our own eight-yard line, Simms passed to the right to Manuel, who fumbled. Rams' linebacker Mel Owens recovered at our six. Three plays later, Dickerson ran one-yard off right tackle for a touchdown. I was moving to my left, had a bad angle, stuck out my left arm, and Dickerson ran through it. I had hyperextended my elbow on the first play of the game and could not flex and extend it. I saw that Dickerson had built up a head of steam. I thought about trying to submarine him. But I didn't want to get another concussion—not that early in the game.

Lawrence Taylor, Kenny Hill, and Perry Williams converged on him at the goal line, but Dickerson made it in. Mike Lansford's kick put us behind 7–0. "I thought we had him stopped," Hill said. So did I. Part of Dickerson's body was over the line but the side that the ball was on did not break the plane of the goal line. I told the official so, but he had his mind made up. We also thought the Rams were in an illegal formation on all three plays because their tight end was lined up off the line of scrimmage. On their touchdown, we thought their wingback was illegally in motion. The officials didn't agree. I'll tell you, it's really disorienting to have to run back on the field right away after a turnover. Bill Belichick had just summoned the defense to a huddle on the sideline when we heard shouts of "Defense! Defense!" and had to get back out there.

At the start of the second period, the Rams drove 66 yards in 13 plays, consuming 6:31, but we made them settle for a 31-yard Lansford field goal which made the score 10–0. The Rams crossed us up. Kemp completed three first-down passes during the drive, and Dickerson ran six times for 39 yards. But our linebacker, Byron Hunt, made a critical sack of Kemp that really emphasized Byron's value to our defense. It probably was the most athletic play of the game. He defeated his blocker, ran full-speed to his left, and sacked Kemp. Byron became a starter after Banks was hurt. Byron has been in and out of the starting lineup since his rookie year in 1981. He's the kind of player who needs time to warm up. He doesn't perform well coming in cold.

During the 1985 preseason, Byron was expecting a trade. He knew Lawrence would go all the way at outside-right linebacker and the Giants projected Banks as the left-side starter. With Andy Headen around for use as a designated pass-rusher, Byron figured the only way he'd get in was after an injury. Byron was looking forward to a trade, possibly to Houston, because he wanted to be a starter. But I think the Giants realized Byron was too valuable to get rid of. I was glad they kept him.

Our offense was not getting much done. It moved from our 24 to the Rams' 32, but on third down Simms was sacked for an eight-yard loss, putting us out of field goal range. The Rams got the ball back at their own 11 and moved right back down the field. On second and seven, Dickerson was stopped cold on a run off right guard and Curtis McGriff tried to wrestle the ball away from him. We thought Curtis had it. Our players were running around, complaining to the officials. That's what we are taught to do—create commotion to confuse the officials. But it didn't work. I called a time out, hoping to settle everybody down.

On third-and-seven, we put in our nickel defense: a four-man front, two linebackers, and five defensive backs, expecting a pass. Instead, Kemp handed to Barry Redden on a draw play. It caught us by surprise. I wasn't in the game. I watched Redden fake inside and circle left end and break into the secondary. Kinard had a clear shot at him and missed. Herb Welch had to tackle him from behind after a 41-yard gain. It was a good call by the Rams. It surprised us. It's a chess game sometimes.

On the next play, Kemp hit Henry Ellard on an 18-yard slant to our 27. If we had let them score a touchdown here, we would have been in big trouble. Luckily for us, the Rams got conservative. They ran Dickerson right and Dickerson left for two yards apiece. On third down, tight end Tony Hunter dropped Kemp's pass. Lansford came out and kicked a 40-yard field goal to make it 13–0.

At this point there was a lot of bitching and complaining on the field. Taylor started to come down on Elvis Patterson because Elvis was getting beaten on quick slant passes. Then Jim Burt defended Elvis. Jim and Lawrence almost came to blows. Elvis was playing cautiously because he had to respect the speed of Ron Brown and Bobby Duckworth. Lawrence thought Elvis was giving them too much room. I called the defense together and told everybody that we play together, regardless of what happens, and we never belittle or berate our teammates. That was directed at Lawrence.

We got the ball back with 1:13 left in the half. The crowd was restless, but then we finally caught a break. On third-and-four at our 26, Simms handed to Tony Galbreath out of a shotgun formation. Galbreath was stopped two yards short of a first down, but the Rams were whistled for a five-yard facemask penalty, giving us a first down.

We had 42 seconds left and were 67 yards away from a score. From the shotgun, Simms passed 24 yards to Manuel on the right. Then he hit McConkey with a quick-out to the left for seven. We were at the Rams' 36, with 27 seconds left. Simms rolled to his right and threw back over the middle to Bobby Johnson. Johnson cut to his left and outraced Johnny Johnson and LeRoy Irvin to the corner of the end zone for a touchdown. Schubert's kick made it 13–7. That gave us a big lift going into the dressing room.

"If we don't score there," Johnson said, "they come out in the second half with Dickerson left, Dickerson right, and the next thing you know, there's no clock left. It's 0:00."

The score buoyed Simms' confidence. "When we came in at halftime," he said, "we knew what we were doing was the right stuff. We didn't have to change anything. We just had to execute."

At halftime, Burt took me back into the weight room and told me what had happened with Taylor. Burt felt Taylor was putting himself above the team and it wasn't his place to come down on Elvis. I asked strength coach Johnny Parker to tell Lawrence to come back so I could get his side of the argument. I reiterated to him what I had said on the field. At first, he reacted as a hothead. Then he calmed down. He realized it was not a personal thing, that we were still friends. I just did not want him causing Elvis to lose his confidence. Then I told the team I didn't care how much money anybody made we should never belittle a teammate in front of our opponents. I think everybody got the message.

Elvis came up to me and apologized for allowing those slants. I told him, "Never say you're sorry. Just try to do better." I also told him I'd try to drop off and give him some help on those plays. I think the public has a mistaken notion that anybody who plays in the NFL is a thug, an assassin, or a potential psychotic killer. I'm not saying we're all angels. But there are a lot more nice guys in the game than there are bad ones.

In my ten years, I only really saw two good locker room fights: Gary Jeter–Dwight Scales and Gary Jeter–Odis McKinney. Jeter was a nice guy but he had a habit of saying personal, sarcastic things to teammates. Then, if somebody said something back to him, he got upset. I remember Odis was kidding Jeter one day on the way out to practice. Jeter didn't like it and they fought. And even though Jeter had three inches and 85 pounds on Odis, Odis defended himself and fought Jeter off. The same thing happened with Scales. Jeter found himself knocked into a locker, looking up at Scales.

But teammates usually are not at each other's throats. Especially during the regular season. Sometimes tempers flare in training camp, though. Burt usually gets into something with somebody. The offensive linemen are taught to hold, to protect the quarterback at all costs. Sometimes in camp, players hold Burt. Then he gets frustrated, grabs a facemask or throws a punch. Burt and our former center Ernie Hughes got into it every summer.

The coaches don't encourage fighting. But they don't seem to mind it, either. They like manifestations of aggression. I don't like to see teammate against teammate during a game, and I let the guys know that. A basketball coach doesn't berate a player during a game right after he misses a free throw. He waits until after it's over.

On the second play of the second half, Simms faded to pass and under pressure had to unload the ball too quickly. The ball was underthrown and the Johnson intercepted and returned it to our 35. The first time Kemp tried to pass to Brown in the second half, Taylor and Patterson were both in Brown's face and the play gained only two yards. That was nice to see. Soon after that, a 21-yard slant pass to Hunter, with nobody near him, gave the Rams a first down at our 12. But on third-and-seven, Kemp overthrew Ellard in the end zone. We forced them to accept another Lansford field goal, this one a 26-yarder.

The next time we got the ball a 49-yard pass from Simms to Galbreath set up Schubert's 40-yard field goal to close the Rams' lead to 16–10. It was a great play by Tony, whose role is to enter games on obvious passing downs and catch passes coming out of the backfield. He caught a short pass over the middle, stutter-stepped past two defenders, faked Nolan Cromwell to the outside, and cut inside. Tony is a shrewd runner. He makes people miss tackles in the open field. He gets very few chances to play, and he makes the most of his chances.

We were drafted in the same year. I remember playing against him when he was with the New Orleans Saints. He and Chuck Muncie were the best backfield in the NFL at the time. Tony stayed straight and had a productive career; Chuck got into drugs.

Galbreath came to us in a trade before the 1984 season. During training camp in 1985, Tony was nervous about making the team. Coach Parcells asked me to talk to him and tell him not to worry. He sensed that Tony was pressing because we had a good-looking rookie named Lee Rouson who was after his job. But the Giants found a way to put Rouson on IR for the year and get another year out of Galbreath. We were glad to have him.

After we got to within six points, our defense then held the Rams on three downs. They had a third-and-1 at their own 29 and gambled. Kemp overthrew Hunter, who was double-covered deep. On the ensuing punt, Gary Reasons leveled the Rams' Shawn Miller with a devastating, legal, blind-side block. The two were running in opposite directions and Gary caught Miller from the side. Miller fell to the turf and just laid there, motionless, like a dead gladiator. The crowd loved it.

The first thought that went through my mind was, "better him than me." You really can't feel sorry for anybody on the field, even if it's a teammate. You have to remain detached. You can't let your emotions take over. If they do, you'll start fearing for your own safety. That's when you get hurt. I usually don't concern myself with injured players. I just go over to the sidelines and talk to Belichick about what we're doing on defense.

Now our offense really started clicking. Starting at his own 41, Simms passed 26 yards to Manuel on the right, then evaded a sack, rolled to his right and floated a pass to Mark Bavaro for 14 more. Morris carried on four of the next five plays, scoring on a one-yard pitch to the right. Schubert's PAT put us ahead, finally, at 17–16.

In the fourth quarter we had another good defensive series. The Rams started at their 15. A Ram penalty and a sack by Marshall pushed them back to their three. After Dale Hatcher's short punt we took over at the Rams' 30. The momentum had turned.

A pass-interference penalty on Irvin gave us a first-and-goal at the Rams' four. Two plays later, Morris broke through right guard for three yards and a touchdown. Schubert's kick put us ahead, 24–16.

"I didn't think it was pass interference," said Irvin, who hit Johnson after a pass by Simms. "It dictated the outcome, helped them win, but it was a judgment call and I just have to go with it." Irvin claimed he had gone for the ball.

"He was running up my back," Johnson said.

Field judge Bill Stanley agreed, saying, "The defender was not looking for the ball when he bumped the receiver."

On the ensuing kickoff, the Rams' Ron Brown fielded the ball on a bounce at his goal line, faked out Robbie Jones, bounced off Patterson, ran outside Taylor and down the left sideline. Schubert tried to but couldn't run him out of bounds, but did throw Brown off-stride. Headen, on a great athletic play, ran Brown down from behind and tackled him at our 11-yard line. The first thing I thought of was that if we had Flowers, the Rams would not have gotten such a big return.

"He (Schubert) got me just enough to slow me up," Brown said. "It took an important step away. I needed that step to go all the way. I would have, too."

Once again, the pressure was on our defense. The Rams ran Dickerson to the right for five yards. Then they pitched to Dickerson running right again. Hunt and Kenny Hill came up to stop him for a two-yard loss. It was third-and-seven at the eight. Kemp dropped back and passed to Duckworth in the left corner of the end zone. As Duckworth leaped to catch the ball, Hill hit him. Back judge Tom Kelleher ruled that Duckworth had come down with one foot out of bounds, so the pass was incomplete. Kelleher said Duckworth would have been out even without Hill's hit. It was a big break for us. In came Lansford to kick a 25-yard field goal. We still led, 24–19, with 9:14 left in the game.

"We couldn't get touchdowns today," Rams' coach John Robinson said. "We got threes. Those guys in the blue uniforms are pretty good."

Robinson had charged down the sideline after the Duckworth call and screamed that Hill's hit had caused Duckworth to come down out of bounds. "In a game this tight," he said, "the official shouldn't be the one being interviewed after the game. . . . It was the kind of call that goes to the offense 99 percent of the time. If Bobby got it, we would have been playing for a field goal near the end to win, so it was big."

This kind of situation won't happen in 1986. The NFL owners voted 23–4–1 to use an instant replay system this season. The league will have a replay official stationed in each press box. Officials on the field will ask him for help as needed. Penalties will not be a part of the plan, only plays governed by the sidelines, goal lines, end line, and line of scrimmage. I think this system is long overdue and makes sense. It worked in the USFL. I've seen a lot of calls go against the Giants that shouldn't have—and vice-versa. But just for the record: I thought Duckworth should have been credited with a touchdown.

The Rams got the ball back twice after that but we stopped them both times. With second-and-10 at his own 32 and four minutes left, Kemp found Hunter wide open at our 37 along the right sideline. The ball hung. No one was within 15 yards of Hunter.

"I was saying, 'God help me,'" said Patterson, who was supposed to have covered Hunter.

"Everybody on the sideline tensed up," said Bobby Johnson. "Everybody's mouth was wide open. Galbreath said he wanted to go out there and bat it down himself."

Hunter dropped the ball.

"God," said Patterson, "thank you, very, very much."

I think my whole body went numb for a second as I watched that play. I started to feel sick. But then I saw Hunter drop the ball and I felt we were really lucky. The Rams punted two plays later. Their last drive ended when Kemp's desperation pass for Michael Young deflected off Young's hands to Kenny Hill for an interception at our 48.

We won our fourth game in a row for the first time since 1979. Our 7–3 record was our best after 10 games since 1968. We held the Rams under 300 yards, the eighth time in 10 games this year. Dickerson gained 101 yards on 24 carries, but he earned every yard. We knew the Rams were like the Bucs. They want to stretch the defense, look for a lane, and cut back with Dickerson. Our guys played a solid, disciplined game.

"We were stringing out those wide plays he likes," Burt said. "We didn't give him any cutback holes. We were laying some helmet on him. . . . I don't care what anybody says. That was our best defensive effort of the season. We made the plays when we needed to."

"The Giants are the type team," Dickerson said, "that doesn't make any specific adjustments for any running back because they have such a good front seven. They have guys that can control an offensive line. We've played teams this year where there was no way they could stop us without putting eight men right up on the line of scrimmage. The Giants don't have to do that."

I made only one solo tackle and had three assists in the game. The Rams did a good job of blocking me, walling me off from Dickerson. They were double-teaming Burt with a center and a guard who would then slip off and block me. Sometimes a tackle came down on me. When a play broke to my right, they effectively walled me off from making a tackle when Dickerson cut back. It was frustrating. But with my elbow, I couldn't fight my way to the ballcarrier the way I usually do.

Then I hurt my neck in the third quarter. I'd developed a stiff neck after the Tampa game and aggravated it. It was a play that was whistled dead because the Rams were illegally in motion. Dickerson got the ball, ran up the middle and I hit him head first in his chest and jammed my neck. I could turn to either side, but it hurt. The only therapy was ice. Even though I was not a major factor against the Rams, their veteran tackle Jackie Slater and guards Kent Hill and Dennis Harrah said some nice things about me.

Other voices: "It's hard to imagine Harry playing any smarter than he does now," Harrah said. "He's always played smart. He plays good, solid, hard-nosed football. He's up there with the best."

"He's very quiet on the field," Harrah said, "but a very tough individual and as clean as a linebacker comes."

"I've played against Harry for a few years," Hill said, "and he seldom if ever makes any mistakes. He studies us, plays hard, is real competitive and intense. I know when I play against him, I can't make a mistake. I have to stay low because he's so strong that if you raise up, he puts you on your back. On the field, you don't get a whole lot of conversation. Off the field, he's charming. It's a complete metamorphosis. But that's the way the job goes."

Meanwhile, our team was really happy with this comeback victory and began to think about winning our first division title since 1963. "The only people who lose faith in us are the fans," Simms said. "We don't."

"I'm proud of the guys," Parcells said. "They beat a good team."

"Bill Parcells has molded a team of fighters here," Merrill said.

We've been down so long that what comes around goes around. Parcells has brought in his own type of player. It's like a college coach who inherits players from a previous coach. It takes a few years for him to bring in his own recruits. Bill's getting to the point where he knows his players, how to relate to them, and how to motivate them.

After the game, the team allowed female reporters in the dressing room for the first time in its 61-year history. I don't see what all the fuss was about. This is the 1980s. There are women reporters working for most large newspapers. There were women from the *Los Angeles Times*, *The Boston Globe* and *USA Today* covering this game. The Giants had barred Rachel Schuster of *USA Today* from our locker room in New Orleans. She had spoken to the NFL and our lawyers about it.

"I detest it, absolutely, positively," said George Martin, our player representative and a conservative about a lot of things. "The majority of the players object to it. I don't think a woman's place should be in an exclusively men's place, an NFL locker room. I couldn't be more adamant about it."

After the game I put on a suit and tie to attend a charity dinner at a nearby hotel. It wasn't the kind of thing I usually like to do after a game. But this was for a good cause. It was a dinner for a little girl named Colleen Giblin, who had died of a brain tumor. Her parents had put on a fund-raiser to help in future research of such tumors. Lenny Fontes, our assistant coach, asked me to go. A half-dozen players went. We just signed autographs and mingled with the guests.

Meanwhile, Taylor, who had rushed out of the locker room only to run over some glass in the parking lot and slash one of his tires, came whirling back into the dressing room like a madman. He had no spare.

On my way out to the parking lot, I told Phil Simms' wife Diana to go home without him because Phil needed to get treatment on a bruised shoulder. She wanted to be reassured that he was okay, especially with his injury history. He was.

15 Game No. 11
Washington 23
Giants 21

End of a Career?

MONDAY NIGHT GAMES were a novelty in the 1970s. Players looked forward to them. After a while, the thrill faded. Now most players regard playing on Mondays as an unwanted break in their routines. A pain in the ass. What's more, you have only six days to recover physically to play the following Sunday. But the whole nation is watching, so you want to look good.

When I played badly in our third game of the season in 1980, a 35–3 loss at Philadelphia on a Monday night, I considered retiring. At the time football wasn't much fun. I was tired of doing the same thing day after day for a losing team. I wasn't as intense as I should have been. I missed a lot of tackles in the game because I wasn't concentrating. It got to the point where everything was black.

After that game I took a stool into an empty room and sat alone for several minutes on a stool while coach Perkins told the team how bad it had played. Then I spent 10 minutes closeted alone with Perkins. I suggested that the Giants donate my game check to charity because I had played so badly. I told him I wanted to quit, to go home and get away from football for a while. He told me to wait and come see him the next day at the stadium.

I telephoned two teammates the next morning—Frank Marion and Jim Clack. I also phoned my old college coach, Willie Jeffries. They all urged me not to rush into a decision, to think about it carefully. The next day was a day off. I brought Aja to the stadium with me. Perk did not try to talk me out of quitting. He just told me to make sure of what I was doing. I know he cared about me as a person, not just a player. I'll always respect him for it. I told him about the nagging feeling in the back of my mind that I wanted an Air Force career. He said if that's what I really wanted, he'd put me in touch with the some people in the off-season who might help me.

My two brothers had joined the Air Force and I'd always had a fascination with flying. I was thinking about joining the Air Force Reserve. I eventually found out you need to do that by the age of $27\frac{1}{2}$. (I let the deadline pass in May 1981.) I also found out I had until age 32 to join the Air Force and attend Officers Candidate School. I just wouldn't have been able to fly. It may sound weird, but I really was thinking about OCS as an alternative to playing on a losing football team.

A week after my meeting with Perkins, I visited a psychologist, Frank Ladata, who had worked with the Giants' players for several years. He once gave us some aptitude tests and I did fine in them. We became friends off the field. He helped me realize what my football problem was. I was missing a lot of tackles in 1980 because: (1) I did not want to be there, I was tired of losing, I wanted out; and (2) I was not making the leap from what we were taught in practice to what is expected in games.

In practice we are supposed to simulate tackles. We arrive at a ballcarrier prepared to deliver a blow, but then just wrap him up or touch him on the shoulder. We're told not to leave our feet in practice to strip blockers, not to punish teammates. But I was doing that in games! I was seeing ballcarriers, hitting them but not knocking them down.

I missed a tackle early in the Philly game that year against 6'8" receiver Harold Carmichael, who everybody called "Big Goose." After that, it started to snowball. My mind started to go blank. I was missing tackles and I didn't know why. Ladata and I worked on task analysis. He told me I had to see myself wrapping up ballcarriers and driving them to the turf. I had to visualize two steps ahead in order to get the job done. We also worked on trying to put aside the fact that I wanted to be traded. Perkins told me before the season there was no way I'd get my wish. So I had to forget about it. I had to try to stop feeling like I was being held prisoner. I never have completely gotten rid of that feeling. I always wondered what it would be like playing for another NFL team. But I stopped dwelling on it. Ladata helped me.

*   *   *

Our practices were lighthearted the week before our second Washington game. On Thursday, Parcells' buddy George Tsiolas, a 26-year-old truck driver from Hasbrouck Heights, N.J., climbed on the top of his cab to watch us practice on the grass field outside Giants Stadium. The guy had become a regular.

"I didn't think too much of it when I first saw him," Parcells said. "He was friendly though, and we started talking. . . . Then I noticed when he showed up, we'd win. So I asked him to come around as often as he could."

Parcells has a few crazy superstitions. Like he always starts practice with the ball at the 28-yard line. And he wears shorts to practice—even in the dead of winter. He refuses to call the coin toss before games. He leaves that to me. My college coach, Jeffries, was superstitious, too. He would tape the bottoms of his trousers. Certain guys have other rituals. Guard Chris Godfrey always was the first player in the dressing room for a home game in 1985, at about 8:30 a.m. When he got there, he found Parcells seated on the same chair, sipping a cup of coffee. Parcells asked, "Where've you been."

The next three to arrive were Brad Benson, Karl Nelson, and Dee Hardison, always in that order. Benson always put on his right shoe before the left and right glove before the left. Then Phil McConkey would come in, get taped, read the game day program, and find somebody to play catch. About five minutes before the pregame warmups, defensive line coach Lamar Leachman usually marched through the dressing room hollering, "Let's get it!, Let's get it!," and other inspirational messages. Lamar's the team motivator. He's like an evangelist at a prayer meeting, but he doesn't have any crazy superstitions.

Parcells says he never picks up a penny that's lying tails-up. He had half the organization searching for his lucky sweatsuit in 1984 after Jim Burt hid it. Godfrey always sits on the right side of the plane on our flights to games. I really don't have time for that kind of stuff. To me, the game of football is simple. Being superstitious doesn't help. Either you're going to get your butt kicked or you're going to kick somebody else's butt—that's what it boils down to.

We knew superstitions would not provide us with a victory at RFK Stadium in Washington, D.C. The Redskins always are tough there. It's a small stadium and it seems like there are 150,000 people in there. The Redskins had their backs to the wall at 5–5. If they wanted to make the playoffs, they almost had to beat us. Washington had fallen on hard times. Their injury-riddled offensive line had allowed 18 sacks in the previous four games. Quarterback Joe Theismann had thrown 16 interceptions and only seven scoring passes. He was being booed by his home fans. And coach Joe Gibbs was phasing out John Riggins.

It took every trick in Gibbs' playbook to beat us this time. We felt like the Redskins were pulling rabbits out of hats. Their three touchdowns were preceded by a faked punt and two onsides kicks. They should never have caught us by surprise so many times. But we had an excuse. Instead of leaving on Sunday morning as we usually do for a Monday night game, Parcells decided we would leave at 10:30 Sunday night. He didn't want us to have time on our hands, wandering around in Washington. I thought it was a bad move. I wanted to leave early and pay my own way. He wouldn't let me.

The plane we were supposed to take did not arrive until 11. I already was so tired that I fell asleep in my seat. Soon the plane was rocking and the engines were roaring and I figured we were getting ready to land. Then I heard the pilot say, "We're number one for takeoff. . . . Please fasten your seatbelts." It was 11:45. Then we were fogged out of Dulles International Airport and forced to land at Baltimore-Washington at 12:30. The players were grumbling. Our buses were at Dulles!

Casey Merrill lightened the mood by opening up a can of Redskins' film and showing it on the wall in the baggage claim area while we waited for buses. "You know," Merrill said, "We're dedicated professionals. All the Redskins are sleeping, but we're up studying film."

Some players, including me, began piling in taxis. The rest arrived at our hotel in Arlington, Virginia at 1:45 a.m. It wasn't until about 3 that we were checked in and asleep. Then we had an 11 a.m. meeting on game day. I know this affected us. I don't know why Parcells did this. The same thing happened in 1984 when he flew us out to Los Angeles the day before a game with the Rams. We didn't get adjusted to the time change and we got killed, 33–12. You'd think he would learn from mistakes.

On Washington's first series, I thought maybe we could forget about it and play sharp anyway. I stopped Riggins after a three-yard gain on first down and dropped him after a one-yard gain on a short pass on second down. Then Merrill tackled Keith Griffin after a three-yard gain on a screen pass. The defense felt great.

It was short-lived. The Redskins' Steve Cox faded to punt. Only he didn't. He raised up and threw a wobbly 11-yard pass to Raphel Cherry. First down. Our defense had to go back onto the field. We never expected a fake that early, and we were sluggish.

The Redskins started moving. Theismann converted on two straight third-down passes, to Art Monk and Gary Clark. They had a first down at our 15. Jim Burt jumped offside for a five-yard penalty. Then Theismann threw a 10-yard touchdown pass to tight end Don Warren when we blew the coverage. Mark Moseley's kick put the Redskins ahead, 7–0. Elvis Patterson was on Warren and tipped the ball, but Warren caught it anyway. Elvis told me later he was really tired. He said he would try to do things and his body just wouldn't respond. I told him, "Gee, I thought I was the only one." Elvis' mind probably was wandering because his pregnant wife had been in an auto accident. He had been excused from practice Saturday to be with her.

The score remained 7–0 until Joe Morris slithered through a big hole off left tackle and ran 56 yards for a touchdown later in the period. Eric Schubert's PAT tied it 7–7. Morris has given us an element we have lacked in my Giants' career: explosiveness.

On the second play of the second period, Theismann handed to Riggins and Riggins pitched the ball back to Theismann—a flea-flicker. We were not fooled. Our linebackers all penetrated. I hooked Theismann's arm with mine. If I had made the sack, he might not have been hurt. But he slipped away from me. Lawrence Taylor leaped on his back and Gary Reasons jumped on top. We all heard the sickening snap of Theismann's right leg. Blood spurted through his knee pad.

"You broke my leg," Theismann said.

Lawrence jumped up immediately and signaled for the Redskins' trainer. Taylor clutched his helmet in horror at what we had done. We might have ended a man's career.

"You always pray for everybody not to get hurt badly," Taylor said later.

"Oh, God, it was awful," Burt said. "I heard a pop. It sounded like two helmets banging together."

Theismann was wheeled off the field to a standing ovation. He had suffered a compound fracture of his right leg. You could see his foot just dangling. "It went through me," Taylor said. "I felt like it happened to me. It made me sick."

We all know something like this can happen at any time, even in practice. You try not to think about it. You steel yourself. When it happens, you can't allow it to take your mind off the game. While the doctor and trainer were administering to Theismann, I was on the sidelines asking our coaches what to expect from Theismann's backup, rookie Jay Schroeder. Nobody seemed to know anything about him.

Theismann was conscious. He said, "Harry, who got me?" I said, "It wasn't me, Joe." It was not a pretty sight.

Up in the press box, Lenny Fontes was calling down to Parcells to get us off the field so we would not be exposed to the sight of

Theismann. It's like seeing somebody's head blown off in the battle. You try to shield people from the sight so they don't lose their courage.

We were talking to Theismann, trying to keep him from going into shock. I looked into the end zone and saw a banner that said, THEISMANN'S OVER THE HILL—HE SHOULD GIVE IT UP. I wondered how the banner-maker felt as Theismann was carted off the field and driven in an ambulance to a hospital. Joe told us, "Don't worry, guys, I'll be back." I said, "Yeah, Joe, but you won't be back tonight."

"I was kind of kidding with Joe when I went out on the field," Redskins' coach Joe Gibbs said. "I looked down at him and said, 'This is a fine mess you've left me with.'"

All I knew about Schroeder was he had played baseball at UCLA and was supposed to be scrambler like Theismann. Later, I found out Schroeder had started only one football game in college and left after his sophomore year to play baseball in the Toronto Blue Jays' system. We certainly didn't expect him to walk in cold and beat us. But that's what he did.

On third and 12 at his 43, Schroeder dropped to pass for the first time and rifled a 44-yarder to Art Monk on the right side against Mark Haynes, who was in as an extra defensive back. He had come off the bench and he was cold.

A few minutes later, Haynes told Bill Belichick that he refused to be platooned, saying, in effect, "Play me or bench me." The Giants decided to bench him. It was the only thing they could do. No player is bigger than the team. Mark had felt the coaches turned their backs on him during his holdout. They did. I think the coaches should have kept quiet and just let management work out the situation. But Parcells came out and said the Giants would not trade Haynes and reporters could write it in stone if they wished. Mark did not forget that. It was obvious that his heart was not in his job.

Anyway, Schroeder's first pass got our attention. Four plays later, Washington had third-and-two at our five. "I think everybody was kind of waiting to see what was going to happen," Gibbs said. "Is he going to respond or are we going to take the gas pipe? I was watching and when the ball took off [on Monk's catch], I think everybody on the sideline jumped."

Then we got a break. Schroeder handed off to Riggins running straight ahead. Taylor hit him in the backfield. The ball popped loose. Taylor fell on it at the two. Once again, the momentum had turned. The half ended with the score still 7–7. Our offense had its worst half of the year, gaining only 109 yards. And we were still in the game!

We never expected the Redskins to try an onsides kick to start the second half. That's a tactic teams use at the end of a game when they need a quick score. So Washington surprised the daylights out of us when its onsides kick was recovered by the Redskins Barry Wilburn the Washington 46. It was a gutty call by the Redskins' coaches. The ball was right there for our Robbie Jones but he was not alert and did not fall on it.

No matter how many times I say it, it did not seem to sink in: THE REDSKINS LIKE TO STRIKE DEEP AFTER A TURNOVER! On the first play, Schroeder completed a 50-yard bomb down the right sideline to Monk behind Patterson. That gave them a first-and-goal at our four. I guess some guys never learn, but I was too tired to chew out Elvis.

"It was like a fairytale, really," Gibbs said of Schroeder, "to be thrown into a situation like that and perform like that."

Schroeder scrambled to his right on first down and I tackled him at the one. Then he handed to Riggins. Byron Hunt and I stopped him in his tracks for no gain. But third down Riggins powered off left guard and a touchdown into the end zone. Moseley's kick put us behind 14–7.

It was Morris' turn to work some magic again. Simms completed a 29-yard pass to the right to Mark Bavaro for a first down at Washington's 41. On the next play, Morris got a great trap block from right guard Chris Godfrey, ran straight ahead, cut to his left, and went 41 yards for a touchdown. Schubert's kick tied it. This was one Monday night game fans would be talking about for a long time!

We had become pretty good at trap blocks. On a trap block a lineman vacates a hole, hoping that a defensive lineman steps up into it and is blocked from the side by another player, either a pulling guard or tackle. I think trap blocks are a big reason Morris started running effectively for us, beginning in the second half of the 1984 season.

The next time Washington got the ball, Reasons forced Riggins to fumble for the second time. I can't remember that ever happening before. Kenny Hill recovered at the Redskins' 33. Morris ran for eight yards on first down. But then we gained only one yard on three running plays and turned the ball back over. Parcells passed up a possible 41-yard field goal by going for it on fourth-and-one at the 24. The Redskins upended Morris for no gain. The momentum switched again, but it was not disastrous.

On Washington's first play, George Rogers fumbled and our Perry Williams recovered. It looked like the Redskins were trying to hand us the game. It took three plays for us to go 23 yards. We scored on Morris' eight-yard run off left tackle. Carthon's block sprung him. Schubert's kick put us ahead, 21–14, with 6:06 left in the third quarter.

After an exchange of punts, the Redskins got the ball at our 38. Then Schroeder rolled to his right and hit Clark with a 21-yard comeback pass on the sideline in front of Patterson. A 12-yard pass from Schroeder to Warren set up Moseley's 28-yard field goal, cutting our lead to 21–17.

No problem, we thought. Only now the Redskins successfully executed another onsides kick. Andy Headen failed to cover the ball and Greg Williams did, at our 46-yard line. Our defense had to go back on the field. We were dragging. The lack of sleep was catching up with us.

After three plays, Washington had another first down at our 29. Then, on a run off left guard by Griffin, Terry Kinard was penalized for illegal use of hands. Fifteen yards! On the next play, Schroeder faked a handoff and hit tight end Clint Didier on a 14-yard touchdown pass over the middle. Reasons bought the run-fake to Griffin and could not recover in time to cover Didier. Moseley hooked the PAT to the left but we trailed 23–21 with 8:21 left in the game.

Our defense was sucking wind. The Redskins were running sprint-out plays for Schroeder, which gave him more time to throw and negated our pass rush. Meanwhile, our offense made only two first downs and did not get beyond our 41-yard line in its last three series. The game ended with an interception by Washington's Vernon Dean. Simms was under constant blitz pressure the whole game and did not read it well.

The Redskins got a break when our receiver Phil McConkey was mauled by Washington defensive back Darrell Green on our last series and no penalty was called. We also thought that Dean pushed off in order to make his game-ending interception.

Parcells had warned us before the game not to expect much help from the officials. He keeps notes on the tendencies of various officials. For instance, Ben Dreith is notorious for calling roughing the passer if you just look at a quarterback the wrong way. Some officials are nuts for calling offense holding. For this game we had the ultimate problem. Referee Fred Wyant is a former Washington Redskin!

After the game, I asked him, "Is it true that you once played for the Redskins?" He just smiled. I'm not insinuating that it affected his judgment. Like I said about the Rams' game, these things even out over a season.

This was a demoralizing defeat, because the defense had played fairly well. The Redskins just capitalized on their trick plays and beat us.

"They rolled the dice tonight and the dice rolled their way," our special teams' coach Romeo Crennel said.

Schroeder completed 13 of 20 passes for 221 yards, which was better than Simms' nine-for-18 for 138. Schroeder did not throw an interception and did not take a sack. "He was amazing," Headen said of Schroeder. "It was like he'd been in there all year."

"All of our guys and all of our coaches dedicated the game to Joe (Theismann)," Gibbs said. "I think we found a successor to Joe tonight."

Theismann underwent two successful operations to repair the compound fracture and vowed initially that he would return in 1986, even if he was forced to start it as Schroeder's backup. However, the Redskins released him on July 25, 1986 after he failed their physical. He took a job as a CBS-TV analyst. "My goal is to be able to live a normal life," he said. As a result of the accident, his right leg is shorter than his left.

After the game, a female reporter from UPI was interviewing Leonard Marshall when a few teammates grumbled about the presence of a woman in our dressing room. A reporter from the Howard University radio station defended the woman's right to be there. Words were exchanged between the reporter and Brad Benson. The reporter called Benson "a loser."

Benson rose from his stool and the reporter repeated the word "loser." Carl Banks hustled to the reporter's side and screamed, "Ain't no fucking losers in here. Get out of here!" Other players started converging on the reporter but security guards, our co-owner Wellington Mara, public relations director Ed Croke, and security manager Joe Mansfield broke it up and escorted the reporter away. Sure we were frustrated, but the loss did not mean our season was over. We had five games left. We had to win three to make the playoffs. We were sure we could do it.

16

Game No. 12
Giants 34
St. Louis 3

Alka-Seltzer

THE BIG NEWS the week before our next game was that the Giants had released Earnest Gray. He was claimed on waivers by the Cardinals and would be in uniform for them for our game in St. Louis. Now you see why I don't get close to my teammates. What if Gray and I were best friends and I had told him my weaknesses, my fears, my shortcomings? Then he'd have to tell the Cardinals and they'd have an edge in attacking me. I was sure St. Louis coach Jim Hanifan would pump Earnie about us, anyway. But at least I wouldn't have anything coming back to haunt me. I had never talked much about football with him.

When Earnest had rejoined our team, he was a little rusty at first, but he soon started making good catches in practice. One day he ran deep downfield and a defensive back was with him, stride for stride. Earnest adjusted to the ball in flight, caught it, and made an all-pro play. I yelled to him, "Now, Earnest, you're going to make it real hard for Bill [Parcells]. With catches like that, he'll have to keep you."

It was a strange business decision. The Giants chose to cut Earnie and keep receiver Byron Williams, who had not caught a pass in 29 quarters. They also kept little-used reserve guard David Jordan and reserve defensive lineman Dee Hardison. There was a message here. In cutting Gray, reducing the role of Merrill, and using Mark Haynes sparingly, management was telling the players that holding out always backfires. As if we didn't know.

"I feel I'm as good as any receiver they've got," said Gray of the Giants, adding, "I'm happy to be a Cardinal."

The Cardinals (4–7) were one of the biggest disappointments in the NFL through 11 games. Many reporters had rated them preseason favorites to win our division. But a lot of people had a bad year at the same time. Now they had no chance to make the playoffs.

Coach Jim Hanifan and his staff would be fired at the end of the season. There would be allegations of drug abuse by several St. Louis players. I saw no evidence that any of the Cardinals were stoned or hung over, but they did seem to give up once the game started going against them.

After the season it was reported that at least two Cardinals underwent drug treatment and counseling during the season. An unidentified Cardinal was quoted as saying, "There has been a ring of drug users on this team . . . the situation has gotten out of hand this season." Cards' owner Bill Bidwill later ordered urinalysis tests for all his players as part of their postseason physicals. Forty players refused the tests and were fined $1,000 each. The NFL Players Association says their collective bargaining agreement prohibits such tests. The matter is expected to be resolved in 1986. (The Giants did not make urinalysis a part of our postseason physicals.)

Anyway, this was a great time to be playing the Cardinals because we needed to rebound from our loss at Washington. But I sensed a lack of concern during our calisthenics, so I called a team meeting when we went back into the dressing room before the introductions. George Martin sensed it, too. There did not seem to be much intensity. I think maybe some players felt this was going to be easy. We told the guys to snap out of it. I think a lot of them felt the Cardinals were just going to lay down. Some of them didn't even want to clap hands when we came on the field for calisthenics. I told them that anybody who wanted to be cool and not clap could go back to the locker room.

My fears proved correct when St. Louis took the opening kickoff and marched down to our 22. Finally, we got it together. On first down I batted down a Neil Lomax pass. On second down I dropped a pass that went right through my hands. I don't know how many interceptions I've dropped in my career. A couple of dozen, at least. I guess that's why I'm replaced on most passing downs. I had a little excuse, though. The ball came at me just as I turned to look at the quarterback. I'd dislocated the middle finger on my right hand in our second game against the Eagles. Any time a ball hit my hands after that, I got an excruciating pain in my finger. In practice I started to let the ball hit my body rather than catching it with my hands. I tried to do that in the game and it hit my thigh pad and bounced away.

On third down Elvis Patterson broke up a pass intended for Pat Tilley. We forced the Cardinals to take a 39-yard field goal by Novo Bojovic.

The first time we had the ball, Simms was sacked, fumbled, and the Cardinals recovered at their 42. But our defense gave them three downs and forced a punt. Nothing much happened until an interception by Patterson preceded a 53-yard drive to Eric Schubert's 27-yard field goal. It was 3–3 at 6:29 of the second period.

The next time we got the ball, Lionel Manuel came back to catch Simms' underthrown pass against Cedric Mack, then cut inside Mack and scored a 31-yard touchdown. The half ended with us ahead 10–3. It was still anybody's game. I was a little pissed off because we were making mistakes. The guys were complaining about the cold. I told them to put the weather out of their minds. I'm a little fanatical about blocking out the cold. I don't wear a T-shirt, regardless of the weather. I just rub a coat of Vaseline over my whole body. It's an insulator. One day in practice I wore a T-shirt and George Adams asked me if I was getting soft. But when he saw me going out in St. Louis with no T-shirt, he thought I was crazy.

The second time the Cards had the ball in the third quarter, Lawrence Taylor sacked Lomax and Martin recovered his fumble at the St. Louis 13. That set up Schubert's 24-yard field goal. I committed a holding penalty and the kick was nullified. But luckily for me, Schubert made it from 34 yards and we were ahead 13–3.

I lined up on the right wing on the field goal team. My job was to prevent my opponent from circling outside me to block kicks. I had to block Freddie Joe Nunn coming inside and then bounce back outside and get Leonard Smith. Smith was coming full speed, and I felt if I didn't hook his arm, he'd block the kick. But Schubert was real cool and just made the next one.

St. Louis looked awful. Jim Burt recovered another Lomax fumble at the Cards' 20. Five plays later, Schubert's 28-yard field goal try hit the right upright. We were not exactly devastating on offense, either. During that last series, Manuel suffered a hamstring injury which would sideline him for the last four regular-season games. He was our leading receiver with 49 catches.

Anyway, we stopped the Cardinals again. Then Simms capped a 48-yard drive with a 12-yard scoring pass to Mark Bavaro. Schubert's PAT put us ahead, 20–3. Scott Brunner, an ex-Giant, replaced a battered

Lomax late in the game and did nothing right. It was sad. Scott had taken us to the playoffs when Simms was hurt in 1981. Now he was an ineffectual backup.

Adams scored later on a 37-yard sweep around right end. And Martin capped our rout by catching a tipped Brunner pass at our 46 and running 54 yards for a touchdown. It was George's sixth career score. Martin has been used as an extra tight end in short-yardage situations. One of his TDs came on a pass from Simms. The other five came on defense and are an NFL record for defensive linemen. George and I have been through a lot of lean years together. I know there was a time I did not want to be seen wearing my Giants' windbreaker to the supermarket. I rolled it up and put it in the back of a closet. Now I'm proud to wear it.

Martin is one of the most unselfish players I've ever known. He's a cheerleader. He feels good when other people do well. He's never jealous. He leads our prayer meetings and he's our player representative to the union. He leads us in a special, inspirational way. He's kind of corny, but I love him.

After Martin scored, I ran down the field to congratulate him. I smacked him on the helmet and told him he was making the over-30 crowd very proud of him. It was gratifying that Martin's touchdown capped our most decisive victory in 31 years against the Cardinals and our first blowout of the season. Our defense had eight sacks, three interceptions, and recovered two fumbles. Martin had three sacks and a fumble recovery. It was a nice way to go into the Thanksgiving holiday. Since his first Giants' season in 1975, George and his wife Diane have hosted teammates for Thanksgiving Day dinner. "This party is going to be the most jovial we've had," Martin said. He and I certainly were enjoying being 8–4. We were still tied with the Cowboys for the division lead, and we had a lot of positives.

One of the biggest pluses in St. Louis was that Adams carried 25 times for 113 yards and gave Joe Morris a rest going into the home stretch. Morris had fumbled twice in the first quarter. Adams had fumbled five times in the first 11 games, but he did everything right this game. If he can stay healthy and develop confidence in himself, I think he can be a top-notch back.

Another positive sign was that Lawrence Taylor had his second straight good game. He had suffered a sprained right knee on the first play of the second quarter, had the knee wrapped, wore an Anderson brace during the second half, and refused to allow Parcells to replace him. I think Lawrence figured he'd be better off moving around than sitting in the cold on the sidelines.

I get mistaken for Taylor all the time. I was in a pancake restaurant and a waitress came up to me and said, "May I have your autograph, Mr. Taylor?" I had to disappoint her and tell her I'm Harry Carson. They say all black people look alike. Lawrence and I are about the same size and complexion, but we're different in a lot of ways. Lawrence certainly does not have to worry about somebody taking his job. Other players sometimes do. There is a macho code in the NFL. Players must learn to play hurt. Otherwise they do not last long.

Players react differently to injuries. Simms is very emotional whenever he gets hurt because the first thing that flashes through his mind is that his season is over. Simms failed to finish four seasons in a row from 1980 to 1983, so you can't blame him for overreacting. Other players deny that they are hurt even when they're limping or their arm is dangling. They seem convinced the risk of being hurt worse is a better gamble than loss of esteem in the eyes of their opponent, teammates, and coach. I once refused to come out of a game even after I sustained cartilage damage to my knee. It was against Dallas and I did not want to give the Cowboys the satisfaction of knowing they had knocked me out. I played the second half, then went on the IR list a few days later and underwent minor surgery.

Morris suffered a concussion during our first Washington game in 1985 and became delirious. Our trainer, Ronnie Barnes, asked him where he was. Joe looked around for a minute. He eventually was able to remember his name and phone number and was allowed to reenter the game. Then he collapsed. Barnes hid his helmet after that. There was no way Ronnie or the doctor was going to let him back into the game.

Players often are told by doctors that they have a choice between playing on Sunday and missing the next couple of games or resting a week and being ready sooner. Halftime conferences between coaches, trainers, doctors, and injured players are common. But I've never seen the Giants return a player to a game where that player was in jeopardy of serious injury. And I've never seen a player take a pain-killing injection to mask an injury. That stuff happens only in the movies.

Sometimes, however, the coaches fail to acknowledge an injury. In our first game in 1984 against the Rams, I hurt my rib early in the game. It hurt even to breathe, much less to make a tackle. But Bill Parcells said, "Harry, I need you for one more quarter." Then at halftime he told me, "We need you for one more quarter." It felt good to be needed, but eventually I had to come out and Robbie Jones went in. I guess I'm not suspicious enough to think I was being used as a piece of meat. I feel like the weak-inside linebacker position is mine.

I don't feel anybody can play it better than me. It's an ego thing. As long as I can walk, I want to play. I don't want somebody messing up at my position, so it usually takes something major to get me off the field.

The training staff has to walk a thin line, leaning toward the coaches' side. The trainers are employees of the team, not the coaches. The trainers are not there to be buddies with the players. When a coach is fired, the trainers aren't. When a player is released, the trainers aren't. The trainers keep an injury file on every player. Mine must be as thick as an old bible.

The Giants' film crew, Tony Ceglio and John Mancuso, film all of our practices and save the film, just in case a player wants to sue the team on the basis of an injury he might have suffered in practice. Or a player might want to bring an injury grievance, saying he was released while he was hurt. So the club has a record of all practices on film as potential evidence.

The week before our thirteenth game one of the newspapers had an article which said that in 1985 the average salary for major-league baseball players was $371,000, roughly double that of the average pro football players. The Yankees' average salary per player was $546,000. I know they play 162 games and we only play 16, but I still think pro football players are vastly underpaid. We put our careers and our lives on the line every time we step onto the field. We don't have free agency; there is virtually no movement of free agents. It doesn't seem fair. According to the players union, the Giants were ninth in the NFL in average salary in 1985 and had some glaring inequities.

Our line, which helped Morris to a club rushing record, had four of its five starters earning $200,000 or less: Chris Godfrey ($200,000), Brad Benson ($175,000), Bill Ard ($150,000), and Karl Nelson ($125,000). Defensive end Leonard Marshall ($125,000) was the best candidate for renegotiation; he was to earn a mere $150,000 in 1986. (He would show his displeasure by leaving a May 1986 minicamp.) And Morris earned only $143,000 in 1985, making him thirty-second on our salary scale! (Morris held out, seeking a new four-year, $3.2 million contract during our 1986 camp.)

17 Game No. 13
Cleveland 38
Giants 35

The Defense Collapses

COACH PARCELLS decided to activate rookie receiver Stacy Robinson from the IR list to replace Lionel Manuel. The unfortunate thing was that we had lost Earnest Gray to the waiver wire the week before. He knows our system and would have been able to step right in for Manuel as a starter.

Now we would have to start little Phil McConkey and use Byron Williams as the third receiver on obvious passing downs. Robinson would be just an extra available body in case somebody was hurt. Williams probably is our fastest receiver. He had problems in 1984 with drops but then took a self-improvement course before the 1985 season, which helped him concentrate better. He caught the ball much better in 1985, but we still lack a receiver with blazing speed. (The Giants hoped they might have found one in the 1986 draft, when they took three wideouts in the late rounds. Williams was waived in August 1986.)

The subject of our home fans booing Phil Simms came up during the week. Booing quarterbacks is a tradition in the NFL. Simms was having an up-and-down year. He fumbled 14 times, a club record, in the first 12 games. He was intercepted in the final minutes of two losses. He was accused of holding the ball too long instead of throwing it away when he was under pressure. But as I looked around the NFC I saw nobody really having a better year.

The rest of the players wish the fans would be more patient and understanding with Simms. Some players were perturbed when he was booed during games. But I think Phil just tuned the fans out. We never talked about it with him because it would not serve any purpose. He never discussed it with us.

"It's brutal," GM George Young said. "I'm getting letters to fire the quarterback." Wellington Mara told Young the team had the same problem with quarterback Charley Conerly in the 1950s. Conerly's wife told *Newsday*'s Peter King that Conerly even was booed at a Rangers hockey game in New York.

"It's the easiest position for everyone to judge," Simms said. "People can judge how a quarterback does, but they can't tell if a linebacker did the right thing on every play." That's lucky for guys like me.

I celebrated my thirty-second birthday Tuesday night by going to my management class at FDU. No wild drinking bouts with teammates—I guess I'm just a dull guy.

My teammates threw me a helluva party in 1983. Frank Marion got me to hotel on some pretext. My sister flew in from South Carolina. They decorated a ball room with my baby pictures, high school pictures, and other old pictures. Brian Kelley and Brad Van Pelt arrived with a stripper named Wendy.

The women were asked to leave. It turned into a bachelor party. I'd never been to one so I didn't know what was going on. They sat me in the middle of the room and everybody pulled chairs into a circle. Wendy started dancing around me, taking off one article of clothes at a time until she was down to a G-string, garter belt and heels. But I couldn't get aroused because everybody was watching. She wound up leaving with Casey.

The Thanksgiving holiday came Thursday, which meant that we had a short workout early in the morning and then split up to have our turkey dinner and watch the two pro football games on television. I was expecting my friends, Frank Marion and Steve Parks, to come in Friday and spend the weekend. I had expected to spend a quiet Thanksgiving in New Jersey. Only that morning, Aja called me up and said, "Daddy, daddy, I have a surprise for you." She told me she had something she had made for me and wanted me to drive to her mother's house in Ossining to get it. So I jumped in the car and drove up. When I got there, was I surprised. There were my sisters and my nephews. "You got me," I told Aja.

It turned into a delayed birthday party for me. My sister Loretta knew I always liked dogs but don't have the time to care for one while I'm playing football. In 1984 she got me a little figurine of a dachshund because I had one named Rex as a child. He followed me everywhere. And in 1985 she got me a bulldog figure because that's the mascot at my alma mater, S.C. State. One year, my sister wanted to give me an expensive gift, so she got me a Ferrari—a remote controlled one.

Marion and Parks flew in Friday as planned. Frank is my former teammate who retired after the 1983 season. He runs a landscaping business in Miami. Steve, a former high school football teammate, is an insurance claims adjuster from Atlanta. I know he's a great Hawks' fan, so I got tickets for us for the Nets against Atlanta Friday night at the Meadowlands.

Steve and I went to elementary school together and were Boy Scouts together. We separated for a while. He went to a mostly white junior high. I went to the black junior high. We got back together in high school and were in ROTC together. Steve never was popular with the girls. Me and some other guys had to educate him as to the ways of the world. Curtis Cato and I had girlfriends in the tenth grade. We used to spend a lot of time talking to them on the phone. Steve was not very cool. I remember him saying, "You guys are too young to be in love." He was the kind of guy who always walked around with a rubber in his wallet and never used it. But we stayed friends. I was in his wedding party. He came to my mom's funeral

My mom came to watch me play a few games before she died. One day in 1978 we were playing in Atlanta. I think Steve was there, too. Anyway, I dove for a ball and somebody hit me. I got the wind knocked out of me. I was stretched out on the ground, but the people around my mother didn't say a word. She had had cataract surgery and couldn't see very well. But later she told me it was funny that people were protecting her feelings. She knew I was down. She also knew I wasn't badly hurt.

Anyway, on Saturday before the Browns' game, I took Steve and Frank to our locker room and Steve was taking photos of everybody and getting autographs. Frank was cool. Frank used to be a carouser. I gave him the nickname Stud, because he was one. But by about 1981 he found Christianity. The nickname stood, but it no longer applied. Frank told the veterans that he really missed the camaraderie of the dressing room, although he didn't miss the game. He said once he left everything started hurting at the same time—his back, ankles, toes, elbows, shoulders, neck. But he still was at his lean playing weight of 221 pounds.

The three of us went shopping in the afternoon and bought some boots. Then we came home and watched college football games and built a fire. Real exciting.

That night, I got up at our meeting at the hotel and had the guys howling. Now Curtis McGriff is a 6'5", 270-pound bear of a defensive end who is quiet, minds his own business, and wouldn't hurt a fly off the field. So, naturally, he becomes the butt of a lot of our pranks. Most of them aren't very inventive. You know, somebody will tape a guy's locker cubicle to look like a jail cell. Or somebody might put dirt or shaving cream in a guy's helmet. My favorite one in training camp is to spray the backs of a guys legs and socks with the water pump.

But this time I had a great gag going. I stood up at the meeting and got very solemn. I told Parcells and the guys that one of our teammates was going through a very tough time, emotionally. Everybody got real quiet. I had them. Then I held up the *New York Post* and said the player's name is Curtis McGriff and he's shattered because Plato's Retreat just closed. Everybody cracked up. Curtis was the last guy in the world who would be seen at a high-priced Manhattan restaurant where patrons shed clothes and donned bathrobes.

I was a little worried that we might be taking the Browns lightly. They were co-leaders in their division, and we expected them to come in highly motivated. I knew that we would not be up as high emotionally as we are when we play our divisional opponents. I also was worried that the cold weather might work to the Browns' advantage, since they were relying on workhorse running backs Earnest Byner and Kevin Mack.

We knew nothing about Cleveland except what we had seen on film. It was the same situation as when we played Cincinnati earlier in the season. The Giants had not played the Browns since 1977. They only had one player I was familiar with—Carl Hairston, the former Eagles' noseguard. But Marty Schottenheimer was the Browns' head coach—my first linebacker coach with the Giants. One time, just after I was drafted, Marty drove me to my hotel in Mount Kisco and told me, "If you work at this thing with me, you will be as good as (Hall-of-Famer) Willie Lanier, at least."

When I came up, there no longer was any stigma attached to black middle linebackers. Lanier at Kansas City and Harold McClinton had taken care of that. In the fifties and sixties the NFL was racist to the extent that there were no black quarterbacks and no black middle linebackers. Middle linebacker was viewed as the quarterback of the defense. The prevailing opinion was that blacks were not smart enough to play either position. I was a little scared in my first camp because most teams projected me as an outside linebacker and I knew I'd have to convert from defensive line. The Steelers said if they drafted me, they wanted to make me an offensive guard. Why, I don't know. But I played middle guard my senior year, which helped me make the transition to inside linebacker. The Giants used a 4–3 formation my first three years, and playing middle linebacker wasn't much different from playing middle guard in college.

Marty was the one responsible for drafting me. And he taught me the tricks of a linebacker's trade—the stance, how to move, reading keys, get in the right position to tackle. Some of the things seem simple, but I didn't know them at the time. He taught me how to play on the balls of my feet, not flat-footed. He taught me to keep my shoulders square to the ballcarrier, work my way down the line, ward off blockers by extending both arms or delivering a forearm blow.

Schottenheimer's quarterback, rookie Bernie Kosar, had been booed a lot lately, too. Kosar came into our game with a 2–4 record in six starts, having thrown only four TD passes and six interceptions. The Browns were 4–2 under 35-year-old veteran Gary Danielson, who was nursing a shoulder injury. We prepared in practice for both Kosar and Danielson.

The Browns were relying on Byner and Mack. They were trying to become the first teammates to rush for 1,000 yards in the same season since Franco Harris and Rocky Bleier did it for the Steelers in the seventies.

I expected to play a lot against Cleveland because they are so run oriented. I also was looking forward to seeing Schottenheimer, who told reporters about me, "I didn't teach him anything. I just put him out there and let him play."

I called Marty after the 1983 season, when I had asked the Giants to trade me. He told me he thought I was too valuable to the Giants and that they never would trade me. I guess he was right. I'm still here.

What unfolded was another game in which we got behind early, fought back, then gave it away. Another crushing loss. It's amazing how many close ones we let slip away in 1985. Our defense stopped the Browns cold in their first two series. We scored first. Simms took us 71 yards in eight plays, completing passes of 18 and 26 yards to Mark Bavaro and pitching to Joe Morris for a three-yard TD run.

But the Browns struck right back. Kosar scrambled right twice and threw third-down passes to Ozzie Newsome and Brian Brennan. Cleveland had a first down at our 42. Then Mack ran to the right, broke my tackle near the line of scrimmage and sped down the middle of the field for a touchdown. That was embarrassing. When you miss a tackle like that, you want to hide. It doesn't happen to me often.

I remember being off balance, coming across, extending my left arm, going for his legs, and not wrapping him up. As soon as I saw him break free, I had a real empty feeling. I don't think it was a play I blew because I'm getting older. I think I just didn't get there in time.

Simms threw an interception on our next series. The Browns moved in for Byner's two-yard scoring run. They were helped by a 25-yard pass interference call that gave them first-and-goal at the two. So we were behind, 14–7. It got worse. Simms threw a pass toward the right sideline, Cleveland's Al Gross picked it off and ran 37 yards for a touchdown. We were down 21–7. I didn't panic though. I felt the offense had enough firepower to come back.

Morris got the crowd off Simms' back by circling right end, using a block by Phil McConkey, and going 58 yards for a touchdown. Unbelievably, Schubert missed the PAT to the right. We trailed, 21–13. We started playing better defense after that and gave Simms the ball back with 1:18 to go in the half. He used the clock beautifully. From the shotgun formation, Simms passed eight yards to George Adams, ran Tony Galbreath 13 yards on an inside handoff, and then scrambled up the middle for 12 yards. Then he hit McConkey with an 18-yard pass over the middle to the Browns' 29.

With 20 seconds left, Simms led Bobby Johnson down the left sideline behind Gross, who never turned around to see the ball coming; Johnson scored. Schubert's kick put us behind 21–20 at halftime.

It was amazing that we had outgained Cleveland 294 yards to 148 at that point and were behind! That changed in the third period. Simms took the offense from its 26 to the Browns' 17 and Schubert kicked a 35-yard field goal. We were ahead 23–21.

Schottenheimer replaced Kosar with Danielson late in the third quarter. "It was the coach's prerogative," Kosar said. "He caught me by surprise. When he told me Gary was going in, I said, 'I don't see why.' He said, 'It's my decision and I'm going with it.' You can't question it because it worked out so well."

Two plays before the period ended, Terry Kinard intercepted a poorly thrown Danielson pass and returned it 22 yards to the Browns'

15. Morris ran twice, the second time slanting five yards off left tackle for the score. Now we were ahead, 33–21. We had scored 26 straight points. I thought the game was in the bag. We were pumped up on the sidelines. I was saying, "Now is the time to play like wild dogs."

We didn't. On the Browns' next play, Newsome beat Elvis Patterson down the right sideline on a 29-yard pass to give Cleveland a first down at our 36. After an incompletion, a four-yard loss by Mack on a draw play, and a 12-yard pass to Byner over the middle, the Browns had fourth-and-two at our 28. This was a key play. Mack turned left end for three yards. He just got outside us. By the time our pursuit caught up with him, he had the first down. You could feel a letdown in our huddle. On the next play, Danielson, who was supposed to have a sore shoulder, led Clarence Weathers perfectly down the left sideline behind Perry Williams for a touchdown. Chris Bahr's kick cut our lead to five points, 33–28.

Danielson said about his TD pass, "I was just throwing to a spot. I tried to pick a spot where he might intersect with the pass. That's what happened."

"The injection of Gary Danielson was like an injection of influenza," Casey Merrill said. "His protection was as lousy as it was all day for Kosar but Danielson was throwing balls off his heel and throwing ducks that were complete. He took some hellacious shots. But it didn't faze him. He'd limp and crawl back to the huddle and come back and burn us again. He was the intangible. He was the difference in the game."

"You get on a roll," Browns' tight end Ozzie Newsome said, "and we feel like we could do whatever we needed to do. I don't think they stopped us all day."

Our offense ran four plays and gave the ball back to Cleveland with 6:56 left in the game. Then the Browns converted a series of big plays. Our defense was awful. On third-and-10 at their 20, Danielson hit Weathers over the middle against Elvis for 26 yards. Danielson had Kinard and Andy Headen in his face on a blitz, and he just lofted the ball out there.

"I was one step late," Headen said. "If he'd held it a second longer, he'd never have gotten it off. But he threw it up for grabs and I don't know how he ever got up again after the hit."

"They knew I was hurting," Danielson said. "So they were coming with more guys than we could pick up. I was just trying to lob it down there to my deepest receiver."

Then came Schottenheimer's guttiest call of the game. On fourth-and-two at our 46, Danielson faked a handoff and passed over the middle to Byner, who caught the ball and eluded Taylor's tackle. I ran Byner down from behind. But he gained 26 yards. We were just fooled on the play. "It was a great call by our offensive coordinator," Newsome said.

"I was supposed to run another route," Byner said. "But the defense they ran confused me. I reacted, just kept running and Gary laid the ball out there."

On third-and-three at the 13, Byner smashed off right tackle, carried Gary Reasons forward, and gained four yards. It was amazing how many big plays the Browns made in a row. Then Danielson's first-down pass for Mack was jarred loose by Kinard's hit. It looked like Danielson threw his arm out on the play. Back came Kosar.

"I didn't want to come out," Danielson said. "I wanted to finish it off, but I couldn't throw."

The Browns lined up with two tight ends and Byner as a lone set back. I figured Schottenheimer had put Kosar in to throw a pass, but he handed off to Byner. He faked inside, I got blocked, and Byner eluded Kinard and Patterson to get outside to the right and score. Bahr's PAT put Cleveland ahead, 35–33.

"Gary gets a very big assist on that," Schottenheimer said, "and Bernie got the score."

We got the ball back with 1:47 left at our ten-yard line. Simms was cool. He threw a 13-yard out to McConkey. Fifteen yards were tacked on when Browns' defensive end Reggie Camp leveled Simms after the pass and was penalized for roughing. Two plays later Simms scrambled 17 yards to the Browns' 45. Then he hit Tony Galbreath for 15 yards and Byron Williams on the right sideline for 12.

We had first and 10 at the Cleveland 18 with 45 seconds left. But we had a problem. After catching that 12-yarder, Williams ran out of bounds, slightly forced by Frank Minniefield. We thought the clock had stopped, but it kept running because head linesman Ed Marion said that Williams' forward progress had been stopped before he was driven back out of bounds.

"We put the ball back on the field at the spot of his forward progress," Marion said, "and the clock keeps moving."

Thirty-one seconds elapsed before we realized we had to use our second time out to stop the clock with 21 seconds left. Then Parcells called a run by Rob Carpenter off right guard. He gained one yard. He called our last time out with four seconds to play. Out came Schubert to try a 34-yard field goal. Schubert was 10-for-11 on the season. He thought to himself, "This'll be easy."

Only center Bart Oates' snap was too low. "It was one of those in-between balls," holder Jeff Rutledge said. "I didn't know whether to catch it or let it hit the ground so I sort of trapped it and put it right up. The laces were fine. The lean was fine.''

"Rut got the hold down perfect," Schubert told *Newsday*'s Peter King, "but the snap did screw me up a little bit. Still, I really felt I was going to make it. I hit it good. But I just hooked it. . . . I go two-for-three but that last one lost the game. That's what happens when you're a kicker.''

"I screwed up," Oates said. "I'm not going to sit here and make excuses. I messed up. . . . I'm not very good at this. I'm human.''

Once again, we should not have let the game come down to that field goal. Our offense did its part. The defense did not. We let Cleveland march down the field too many times and score. When Schubert walked into the dressing room, he was depressed. But I told him not to worry about it. I told him we had not lost confidence in him and that he would have other chances to win games for us.

The Browns gave the game ball to their owner, Art Modell, who purchased the team in 1961. Their victory over us was the team's 200th in 25 seasons. There was an emotional scene in the Browns' dressing room. Modell and Newsome hugged. And Schottenheimer told reporters, talking about Danielson, "It's character like that that enables you to be in a game like this and prevail.''

After the game, I stopped into the Browns' dressing room to chat with Marty. "You're wearing your age well," he told me. Only I was hurting inside. He told me he had followed my career and was proud of me and everything I'd accomplished. He said he and his wife were very fond of me. It was nice to hear, but it did not take away the sting of defeat.

Headen said it best. "Now we've got our backs to the wall, that's kind of Giants' history.''

18

Game No. 14
Giants 35
Oilers 14

Momentum for a Showdown

WHEN THE GIANTS made Butch Woolfolk their top draft pick in 1982, most the reporters who covered the team felt it was a wise choice. We needed a halfback to take the pressure off fullback Rob Carpenter, who literally carried us on his back in 1981. The coaches wanted to diversify the offense. Enter Butch, who had rushed for 3,861 yards at Michigan after graduating from Westfield (N.J.) High School.

In his second pro season, Woolfolk set an NFL record with 43 carries in a game and rushed for 857 yards on the year. But the Giants misused him. At Michigan, he was a tailback in an I-formation. The Giants tried to make him into a halfback in a split-back formation. In college, Woolfolk would take pitchouts seven yards deep, read the defense and cut back against the grain. The Giants wanted him to get up in the hole right away. That's a big adjustment. Butch never made it.

He gained a lot of yards in 1983 because Carpenter was an early-season holdout and never got into top shape. But the coaches never really were committed to Butch. They just had nobody else. Joe Morris was a No. 2 pick the same year as Butch. But it seemed that Joe fumbled every time he touched the ball in his first two seasons.

The Giants returned to a fullback-oriented offense in 1984, relying on Carpenter early in the year. But Rob had lost a step, and we weren't getting much out of our running game.

In our second game that year, Butch went up to catch a pass along the right sideline and took a helmet in his ribs from Cowboys' safety Michael Downs. He had to wear a flak vest the rest of the season to protect his bruised ribs. Later in the year, Woolfolk suffered hand and shoulder injuries. When he did get a chance, he seemed to do a lot of faking and running laterally, trying to protect his ribs. The coaches got down on him. He withdrew.

Carpenter went to Parcells and suggested that he give Morris a chance. Joe replaced Butch as the starter in the second half of that season. The coaches put in a series of trap plays to give Morris holes he could see. And Joe started tapping his potential. He gained more than 400 yards in the last eight games, laying the groundwork for his 1985 season. By lobbying for Joe, Rob Carpenter actually was helping phase himself out of the offense, too—a pretty unselfish move.

Rob's a pro. Winning is the most important thing to him. He told reporters, "Each season is a war. You got the soldiers. Some guys are asked to carry the machine guns and some are asked to carry the ammunition. You just go with it. You go with what your leaders tell you. I've carried the machine gun before and now I'm carrying the ammunition." (The Giants traded Carpenter to the Rams for a draft pick in the spring of 1986.)

The juxtaposition of roles was tough for Joe and Butch because they and their wives are friends. Butch spent those last eight games in 1984 playing on special teams. He bit his tongue and never blasted the coaches. He was reading a book called, *Tough Times Don't Last; Tough People Do*. After the 1984 season, the Giants drafted running back George Adams in the first round and traded Woolfolk to Houston. I called Butch and wished him good luck. I told him he was going to a team where he'd fit in better.

It took me a couple of days to focus on Butch and the Oilers because I was really depressed about losing to Cleveland. I went out with Frank and Steve after the game and they kept my spirits up. Every time the conversation turned to the game, I asked them to change the subject. After they left on Tuesday, I started getting the flu. That wore me down.

Woolfolk came into our game with 64 catches for 666 yards and also had 354 yards rushing. So it looked like he was fitting in. During his last year with us, some of our coaches had hinted to reporters that Butch was lazy. I did not buy that. I thought it was more a personality thing between him and Parcells. The week before our Oilers' game, Butch sounded off to a *Houston Chronicle* reporter. "Last year was the worst time ever in my life as far as football's concerned," Woolfolk said. "I don't think I'll ever get over it . . . to say I'm lazy and have no drive, that hurts. A lot of things were written about my character. . . . I'm not as bad as the press made me sound."

One New York reporter had referred to Butch as "Woe-folk." Others had questioned his courage. That's one reason I like *USA Today*. That paper's reporters don't insert opinions. They just report the news. I've seen a player say something from his heart and seen how a writer twisted his words and made him appear ignorant. The pen truly is mightier than the sword. And a player does not have equal access. He can't criticize a reporter in front of millions of people. It seems unfair.

I've had mostly good relations with the press. But I spent the whole 1981 season not talking to reporters. It was nothing they did. I was just tired of seeing my name in the papers. It had been there a lot in 1980, when I considered taking a sabbatical from football. So I just decided to keep mum.

(When Lawrence Taylor arrived at a May 1986 minicamp, he refused to talk to reporters because he did not like the way they handled the reporting of his off-season substance abuse problem. Parcells backed him and told reporters that if they did not leave Taylor alone, he would bar all reporters from the dressing room for the season.)

Some players will use the press, just as the press uses some players, to drop hints about contract talks or a desire to be traded. Agents manipulate the press, too. Reporters think they are getting scoops, but in reality, the agent paints a distorted picture of contract talks to elicit public sympathy for his client. And management, usually in a "no comment" position, looks like the bad guys.

Usually, players don't pay much attention to what reporters write. So nobody felt that Butch was wrong in criticizing the Giants. Butch came to our hotel on Saturday afternoon the day before the game and got a warm reception. I didn't see him. He called me and invited me to dinner, but I was watching Leo Buscaglia on PBS delivering a message on love. I told Butch I couldn't make it. Butch and his wife Regina invited Linda and Joe Morris and a couple of other Giants over.

I guess Butch figured, "Well, that's Harry" when I told him I couldn't go out. But Buscaglia was talking about life, dealing with life, and love. I was making notes about what he was saying. One thing he said was that anything a person has can be taken away from him at a moment's notice. I found that intriguing. I just got engrossed in it. I didn't want to go anywhere. I don't usually. I like to stay in the hotel and relax the night before a game. I don't go out and tear up bars or terrorize women. At certain times, you have to be reminded that you get so wrapped up in the game of life that you take it too seriously and don't live it the way you should. Just like football, it's a game. Win or lose, the sun is going to rise the next day. Life's going to carry on. Whatever disappointments you've had, you get over them.

I was contemplating that when I turned in after our meeting. But I was tired and exhausted when I woke up at 4:15 a.m. on game day and could not get back to sleep. The flu can be worse than a painful injury to a football player because it clouds your mind and affects your concentration. I started worrying that we might have some kind of jinx against us when we play AFC Central teams. Cincinnati scored 35 points on us and beat us. The Browns got 35 and beat us. We certainly were not going to take the Oilers, who play in the same division, lightly.

On the bus ride to the Astrodome, I was thinking about the Oilers' quarterback, Warren Moon. He was the only black starting quarterback in the NFL in 1985. The Giants had appeared to be courting him after the 1983 season, when he became a free agent and left the Canadian Football League. But I thought it was all a publicity stunt. We had just finished 3–12–1 and management had to show some interest in a player with talent. Most local reporters bought it. I'm certain the Giants never seriously considered signing Moon. The price was just too high—like $7 million for five years. They hadn't given up on Simms yet.

Moon wound up not playing badly against us. He stood in the pocket well. He had a strong arm, but his line is young. We got a lot of pressure on him. We played the best first half on offense that I can remember, scoring all 35 of our points.

We took the opening kickoff and drove 80 yards to score on Morris' 12-yard sweep to the right. Joe shook off linebacker Robert Lyles at the 15, linebacker Frank Bush at the 12, and linebacker Robert Abraham at the nine. Then he lunged over the goal line. It was a great individual effort.

The next time we got the ball, we had a 62-yard march which ended with Morris' two-yard leap over center Bart Oates for a score to make it 14–0.

Early in the second quarter, Houston went 80 yards, scoring on former Giant tight end Jamie Williams' two-yard pass from Moon, who completed eight of nine passes in the drive. Parcells yelled at me when I came off the field because I did not call the right defense on the touchdown play.

Bill Belichick was giving me the bump sign, meaning he wanted our cornerbacks to bump their receivers and a linebacker to jam Williams at the line of scrimmage, trying to disrupt their patterns. I had not practiced Friday because of the flu. We had not done any bumping in practice on Wednesday or Thursday in this particular defense. I had asked Belichick before the game if there was anything new I should know about. He said, "No."

So when I saw him signaling bump, I disregarded it. I figured he had made a mistake. But . . . noooooo!. It turned out that we had practiced bumping on Friday when I was sick. Needless to say, I called the proper signal after that.

The Oilers got the ball back quickly when Maurice Carthon fumbled and they recovered at our 27. Moon threw a scoring pass to Tim Smith to tie the score at 14. Smith ran right by Mark Haynes, who was starting his first game in 12 months at left cornerback. Haynes looked bad to television viewers. Actually he had done the right thing in our zone coverage. Safety Kenny Hill was supposed to pick up Smith deep but he did not get there in time. Hill had the flu bug, too, and he looked miserable. I did, too. I wished we had somebody to replace me. I felt awful. But I had to stay in.

We did not make many more defensive mistakes the rest of the day. And the offense kept putting points on the board. We drove 80 yards back down the field and Simms threw a ten-yard scoring pass to Mark Bavaro. Boy, was Simms happy. He did a Jimmy Connors impersonation, boogieing and pulling an imaginary chain with his right hand.

That's rare these days. Most quarterbacks try to be cool. Roger Staubach was the epitome of a cool quarterback. Jim Hart was the same way. Joe Theismann was the only other really emotional quarterback I've played against. He would spike the ball after he scored. As a defensive player, you don't like to see that. As a teammate, I enjoy seeing Phil being demonstrative; I wouldn't like it if he was an opponent. It would give me added incentive to sack him.

Anyway, we kept battering Moon. Gary Reasons sacked him, he fumbled, Taylor beat George Martin to the ball and ran 25 yards to the Houston 11 before being tackled from behind by Oiler fullback Larry Moriarty. I was surprised at old L.T. He must have been tired. Whenever he gets his hands on the ball, we expect him to go all the way. We all kidded him that he must be getting old to get caught from behind by a white guy. And Moriarty told reporters he was playing with a pulled quadricep muscle!

Two plays later, Morris scored again from the two. It was another great day for Joe. He had 129 rushing yards to give him a total of 1,054 for the season. He became our first 1,000-yard rusher since Ron Johnson in 1972. At 5-7, he also is the shortest player ever to gain 1,000 yards. His wife, sitting in the stands with Woolfolk's wife, had to be very proud of him.

After the game Morris stood on a bench and we gave him a standing ovation. Joe broke down. He couldn't say anything. In an eight-game stretch, during which we were 6–2, Morris had gained 785 yards and scored 14 touchdowns. But he was his usual modest self after the game.

"A lot of credit has to go to [offensive coaches] Fred Hoaglin, Ray Handley, and Ron Erhardt," Morris said, "for what they've done. They've changed our offense to make it better for us. For me personally, I'm very happy for what I did, but you've got to realize the guys up front did a lot of it today. They allowed me to get into the secondary before I even had to make a read. . . . and this is why I got the thousand yards. Goodbye."

After Morris' third touchdown, we stopped the Oilers on three downs and they punted. To finish the half, we drove 70 yards, with Simms passing 22 yards for a touchdown to Bobby Johnson 17 seconds before the gun. Eric Schubert's fifth PAT made it 35–14. We felt we had them in our hip pocket but we also remembered what had happened the previous week. We did not want it to happen again. At halftime we were concentrating on playing harder and just punishing them, not letting up, as we had against Cleveland.

On the Oilers' first series of the second half, a 30-yard pass interference penalty on Perry Williams and a 27-yard pass from Moon to Smith helped the Oilers to a first-and-goal at our nine. But we held them. It reminded me of our goal-line stands in the preseason Hall of Fame game against Houston. Near the goal line, you don't try to think too much. You don't want to overreact or out-guess yourself. You want to be flexible, to respond to what develops.

On first down, Haynes tackled Smith after a three-yard gain on a quick pass to the right. On second down, Terry Kinard came up to stop Woolfolk after a three-yard gain on a pass over the middle. Then Mike Rozier tried running off right guard and got nowhere because I was there. I just went right up into the hole and met him. On fourth down at the three, Moon overthrew Williams in the end zone, with L.T. covering. That was some pretty crummy goal-line offense. Bad play selection.

The next time the Oilers got the ball, a 34-yard bomb from Moon to Drew Hill put them on our nine again. Then Moon hit Williams for six yards over the middle. But he followed that by throwing three straight incompletions. On fourth down Moon had to rush his pass because we had good pressure on him and the ball went off Woolfolk's hands. (The Oilers looked so bad that their coach, Hugh Campbell, was fired the next day.)

Later Casey Merrill told reporters tongue-in-cheek that it was hard for us to concentrate in the second half because of the Astrodome scoreboard and replay screen. "They'd flash up the Dallas score and that was distracting enough," Merrill said. "Then they'd flash up the Houston cheerleaders. It was tough enough not looking at those beautiful curves on the sidelines, and then they go and put them on that big screen."

Those cheerleaders were sexy. They had great bodies. A couple of our guys wanted to get their numbers. I know Casey talked to one. She had great breasts. But she wouldn't give him her number. She must've been married.

I don't think cheerleaders really are necessary. The Giants are a conservative organization and have never had them. They don't lead any cheers. The fans lead their own cheers. Cheerleaders are more or less window dressing. If you're winning, I'll tell you, you appreciate them more. If you're losing, you could care less.

After the game, Woolfolk came over to our bus. We had held him to seven catches for 36 yards and two rushes for seven. Probably his worst game of the year. But I told him we had really been impressed with him on film.

We got word that Dallas had lost to Cincinnati, 50–24. It was one of the Cowboys' worst beatings in their 26-year history. We had hoped after our first Dallas game in October that our second meeting would mean something. Now, it would.

"This is winner-take-all," Parcells said. "I haven't had that experience before. Neither have most of these guys." Both teams were 9–5. The winner most likely would win the division title and get the home-field advantage in the playoffs.

Game No. 15
Dallas 28
Giants 21

Another Bizarre Play

ON MY DAYS OFF, I try to get away from football. The Tuesday before the Dallas game, I decided to go to Aja's school. I had made her a promise earlier in the year that I'd do it. I asked her teacher and she said they'd be delighted to have me. I was educated in a segregated public school in South Carolina. If we did anything wrong, we'd get a strap on our rear ends or our hands. Aja goes to a disciplined school, too, a Catholic school where all the kids wear matching uniforms. She was in first grade in 1985.

I walked into her class and all the kids said in unison, "Good morning Mister Carson." I sat at a little desk. The teacher called the roll and told stories and told the kids what they were going to do that day. After a while, the principal came by and kidnapped me and Aja, who became my tour guide. We went from class to class telling the kids about the importance of education, especially the older ones. The school went from kindergarten through sixth grade. Aja was thrilled by the whole thing. She was subdued, but I knew she was thrilled. I received a lot of compliments from teachers about her being thoughtful and considerate and sharing. That thrilled me.

We had lunch and all the little girls wanted to sit next to me. The boys were a little shy. I spent the day there because I wanted to make sure she's getting a good education and I wanted to show the teachers and the principal that I care about what she's learning. I had a lot of fun and it took my mind off our biggest game of the year.

The mood of the team was relaxed this week because even though we had lost to Dallas early in the season, we felt we were a better team. We had won some games and had momentum. We were quite restrained with the press. I could detect that some reporters were trying to stir things up, but everybody handled it well. We wanted to let our actions speak for themselves and not get into any verbal confrontations.

The buildup for this game was unlike any that I've been associated with as a pro. We had 57 reporters and cameramen in the dressing room on Wednesday, when the press and television get a half-hour for interviews during the lunch break. We went out of our way to say nice things about the Cowboys. And there wasn't much negative about us coming out of Dallas this time, either. Neither team wanted to give the other an emotional edge.

I grabbed an aerosol can of foot spray and sprayed a crowd of 13 reporters around Gary Reasons. I told Gary the spray was to keep him from putting his foot in his mouth. Center Bart Oates was much in demand this week because reporters wanted to rehash his bad snap that cost us the first Dallas game. Oates' locker neighbor Billy Ard leaned over and asked, "What are you going to do for an encore?"

"Two of 'em," Oates replied.

Later in the week, Oates confessed that he had felt very low after that game in October. "As a player in a team sport," he said, "I felt like I'd let down the entire team. I make that one bad snap and with the turnover, all they had to do was kick a field goal to win. I think I have a little better resolve to come back and do better. I plan on playing this game with a lot of emotion, with a kind of controlled rage."

The Giants placed Mark Haynes and backup quarterback Jeff Hostetler on the injured reserve list this week with hamstring injuries, activating rookie running back Lee Rouson for use on special teams and veteran tight end Don Hasselbeck, in case Mark Bavaro couldn't make it. Bavaro had suffered a slight ankle sprain in practice Friday.

We flew to Texas gunning for a chance at our first division title since 1963 and a chance to break a 15-year stranglehold by Dallas and Washington on first place in our division. Before we left, I told reporters that I'd like to be able to say on Sunday night what Jesse Jackson said: Our time has come.

Nobody had to fire us up. We didn't need team meetings or goal-setting or inspiration from the Bible. Everybody knew what was at stake. We just wanted to get it on.

"This is Army–Navy," said Phil McConkey, the Navy man.

"This is UCLA–USC," said Herb Welch, a UCLA alum.

This was the Super Bowl to me. I figured that if we did not win the division this time, I might not be in this position again. We were 9–5 in 1984 and then lost the last two games. I didn't want that to happen again. We really hate Dallas because they perceive themselves to be above the rest of us in the NFL, "America's Team." We don't hate them as individuals, but we hate that mystique. They're on their high horse and we wanted to knock them off. Personally, I prepared myself to try to be a major factor in the game. I made sure I was well-rested. I knew I would be playing a lot. During the week, Parcells decided we would not be playing our "sub" defense much against Dallas but would stick with our starters.

Before the flight down, I picked up a copy of *Sports Illustrated* and saw an article on our general manager, George Young. So I went up to George and asked him to autograph it. I was really busting his chops. He finally broke down and gave it to me. Then I went to the back of the plane and gathered up as many *Sports Illustrated*s as I could find and sent players up one by one to get his autograph. George Martin went up, then Joe Morris and Phil Simms. We all got a kick out of it.

Every year when we go to Dallas, Byron Hunt's friends bring a buffet of barbecued ribs, sausages, potato salad, cole slaw, and beer to our hotel on Saturday afternoon. Byron went to SMU in Dallas. We all got together this year in Byron's room and munched out. Two years ago, Bob Ledbetter, our running backs' coach, had joined us for ribs in Byron's room. Two days later he developed an artery blockage, later diagnosed as a stroke. Eventually it killed him.

Ledbetter, 49, left a wife and 10-year-old son, who had been our ball boy at camp. Bob was a great communicator, a positive reinforcer, and a fine coach. Bob was given credit for helping the Jets win the 1979 NFL rushing title. We wore black arm bands in his honor for the balance of the 1984 season. Our franchise has had more than its share of adversity.

Our owner, Wellington Mara, Cowboy coach Tom Landry, and their wives went out to dinner on Saturday night, as is their longtime custom. Landry was once a Giants' assistant coach and the two have remained friends. It's nice to see that sportsmanship still is a part of the game.

"In the old days," Mara said, "when we trained at Bear Mountain, the four of us used to play bridge together. It was a much smaller, intimate operation."

The next day the locker room was subdued, quiet, intense. We knew what we had to do. No blaring music. We hoped we were getting ready to play the game of our lives.

We held the Cowboys to one first down in their first series and forced a punt. Our offense went out. On third-and-six at our 24, McConkey broke into the clear down the right side of the field. Nobody was near him. Simms threw him a perfect pass. McConkey dropped it. And this is a guy that had fielded 65 punts without a muff. "I catch a hundred of those in a row," McConkey said. "I sure picked a lousy time to have that one bad one happen." I remember thinking about this time: Where is Earnest Gray?

The next time Dallas got the ball their quarterback Danny White took a hit that bruised his left shoulder after unloading a screen pass. He was replaced by Gary Hogeboom. On third-and-26 at our 42, Hogeboom threw a bomb down the right side to Mike Renfro, who got behind Ted Watts. Welch caught Renfro at the five. Watts jumped on his back and poked the ball away. It rolled into the end zone. Our guys didn't see it. Renfro did. He dove on the ball for a touchdown. Rafael Septien's kick put us behind 7–0.

Early in the second period, Simms made a big play for us. On third-and-12 at our 45, he stepped up in the pocket and hit McConkey over the middle. McConkey was coming from right to left. He faked Dennis Thurman and ran down the left sideline, forced out of bounds at the Cowboys' seven. Two plays later, Simms threw a touchdown pass to Bobby Johnson. Eric Schubert's PAT tied the score, 7–7.

On Dallas' next series Elvis Patterson picked off a Hogeboom pass and returned it to the Cowboys' six. Three plays later Simms hit Tony Galbreath over the middle for a 10-yard touchdown and we went ahead 14–7. We put that play in just the previous week in practice. Tony stepped up, Phil faked a draw play, Tony slipped out into the clear, and Phil tossed him the ball.

We held the Cowboys. I didn't get suckered on a reverse they tried with receiver Gordon Banks. We knew that Banks was primarily a kick-returner and if he was in for an offensive play, we had to watch for a reverse. We scouted that play during the week, meaning we simulated it in practice.

Our offense got the ball back and Simms drove us from our 20 to the Cowboys' 22. We had a first down. There were two minutes left in the half. We were in the driver's seat. At least that's what we thought. Then fate cheated us. Simms faded to pass. He was looking for George Adams, who was open at the eight. Cowboys' lineman Ed (Too Tall) Jones, who is 6'9", put up his hands and deflected the ball high in the air. It came down in the hands of defensive end Jim Jeffcoat, who ran it 65 yards for a touchdown. All of us just stood there with out mouths open. Why do these things always happen to us? "If Jeffcoat had beaten me," our left tackle Brad Benson said, "he would never have had the chance. He was four yards behind Phil. I pushed him right into the damn ball.''

Too Tall and I have vacationed together a couple of times. He sleeps all day and parties all night. He doesn't bother anybody. Kind of softspoken off the field. The years might be catching up with him, but he can still move. He read Simms' pass perfectly, put up those big arms, and got the deflection. Instead of us going ahead 21–7, the score now was tied, 14–14. The Texas Stadium crowd was going nuts. ''When they got the ball back,'' White said, ''they weren't the same offense.'' We were dominating the Cowboys, they got a lucky break, and now we all felt empty inside.

I thought to myself that God must wear a Cowboy hat. Their team just wasn't that good. Their defense relies on the blitz a lot because they can't cover in man-to-man defense. And their quarterbacks are fragile guys who are not good leaders. But good things seem to happen to them, anyway.

We took over at our 20. Simms was sacked twice. An inside handoff to Galbreath went nowhere. Dallas took a time out. We had fourth-and-18 at our 12 with 1:12 left in the half. Sean Landeta dropped back to punt.

Before the snap, a thought flashed across my mind. What if his punt was blocked? What if the snap went over his head? You always think about the worst things that can happen.

The snap was a little high. The Cowboys got a good rush. Landeta saw that he would not have time to get his kick away. He should have fallen down in the end zone and let the Cowboys tackle him for a safety. Or taken a two-step approach and tried to get the kick away. Instead, he panicked, shovel-passing the ball forward like a hot potato. It fell incomplete. I just could not believe what was happening. ''We were dominating them in every phase of the game,'' Casey Merrill said, ''and then, wham, bam, and we're behind.''

Dallas took over at our 12. Our defense ran back on the field. White was back at quarterback. On the first play, with George Martin in his face, White hit Renfro behind Elvis Patterson in the right corner of the end zone for a touchdown. Septien's kick put Dallas ahead, 21–14. We were demoralized. We had had the ball for most of the half and we were behind! ''After that play,'' Jones said, ''the momentum shifted. It was a confidence-builder for us, and you could sense it leaving the Giants.''

A good team overcomes mistakes like that. I told the guys at halftime we were capable of coming back, if we didn't beat ourselves. There was no finger-pointing, no yelling. We knew we were better than

Dallas and we just had to eliminate mistakes. On our second series of the second half, Simms took us from our 47 to the Dallas 17. On third down, he threw over the middle for Johnson and Michael Downs intercepted at the nine. We had blown another great scoring chance.

After that the Dallas defense toughened. But early in the fourth quarter we moved into position for a 42-yard field goal by Schubert. Parcells elected to try a fake. It had worked against the Bengals, but not this time. Holder Jeff Rutledge was tackled from behind by Downs for a three-yard loss before he could pitch to Schubert. A field goal would have moved us to within four points at 21–17. The play failed because we could not hear Rutledge's signals over the crowd noise. We didn't know the side that Dallas was overloading. I was lined up on the right wing, and that was the side Dallas had overloaded with more people, hoping to break one in for a block. Our play was going to the left. But I could not hear the call and failed to block Downs. He ran Rutledge down from the back side.

The NFL will experiment in 1986 with an electronic system that will prevent crowd noise from being a factor. So-called "Star Wars" helmets, with miniature microphones in them, were to be issued to quarterbacks and defensive captains in some preseason games. The rest of the players will have small speakers in their helmets. If crowd noise becomes a factor, an official on the sideline will activate the microphones. I think this is a great idea and should become a permanent part of games. I know in our Washington Monday night game the noise was so loud we sometimes couldn't even hear ourselves in the huddle, much less in our formations. We had to resort to hand-signals. We later decided to use hand signals in our season-ending playoff game at Chicago.

All the technology in the world would not have helped in Dallas after Jeffcoat's touchdown. Late in the game, Tony Dorsett was running like he was shot from a cannon. He was coming off the ball well, hitting holes, and scooting by us before we could get off our blocks. The Cowboys were playing hungry. Hogeboom had followed White to the sidelines after taking a blow to the head from Perry Williams in the third quarter and suffering a concussion. But Dallas' third-stringer Steve Pelluer directed a 72-yard scoring drive to clinch the game. He never had thrown a pass in an NFL game!

It was just like with the Redskins' quarterback, Schroeder. We had no scouting report on Pelluer. Then he completes the biggest pass of his life on third-and-15 at his own 48. Beating Lawrence Taylor's blitz, Pelluer found rookie Carl Powe over the middle for a 28-yard gain. The Cowboys alternated running Dorsett and Timmy Newsome on the next five plays. They went through us like a sieve. On third-and-one at the

15, Dorsett circled right end for 10 yards. Two plays later, Newsome ran one yard for a touchdown. That put the game out of reach, 28–14. For the second week in a row, our defense failed at a key time.

We managed a 73-yard drive, capped by Morris' one-yard scoring run, but it was too little, too late. We got the ball back at our 39 with 1:37 left in the game. Simms threw a deep post to Byron Williams over the middle for a 45-yard gain to the Cowboys' 16. But two incompletions and a sack by Randy White brought up fourth-and-18 at the Dallas 24. Then Simms threw a pass for Williams on the right sideline. Dallas' Victor Scott intercepted and we were done. It was one of the most crushing defeats I ever have had to accept.

"Every time we play those guys," Taylor said, "we beat ourselves."

"It was the toughest loss of my career," George Martin said.

After the game a reporter suggested to Simms that some fans would think the Giants had blown another big one. "Those people can go to hell," Simms said. "You can print that. Nuts to those people! I played my ass off and. . . . I'm proud of myself and proud of this team! All that about big games and we can't damn win them. I'm tired of reading that baloney. And that's the end of the interview."

We had more first downs than Dallas, 25 to 13. We had more plays, 84 to 61. We had more yards, 396 to 273. And we still lost. I told the reporters afterwards that I wasn't devastated, but I really was. To say our backs were to the wall was an understatement. We had dented the wall.

"I'm upset most," Leonard Marshall said, "that I missed a shot at history."

So was I. I've never played on a division title winner. Our team goal was to win the NFC East. And we had failed.

The mood on the flight home was surprisingly jovial. We knew we had outplayed them. We knew we were a better team. We had just gotten beat, so we tried to put it out of our minds. Dwelling on the missed opportunity would not help us get ready for our regular-season finale against the Steelers. We knew we still had a chance to make the playoffs as a wild-card team if we won our last game.

20 Game No. 16
Giants 28
Pittsburgh 10

Morris Carries Us into the Playoffs

I DON'T KNOW why the schedule-maker had us playing a Saturday home game four days before Christmas. On Wednesday it was bitter cold. "When I got home," Phil Simms said, "I almost passed out. I don't remember being that cold." The temperature was about 20 degrees, but the wind-chill made it feel like below zero. I was playing Superman. I just put vaseline on my body and went out in my normal practice uniform and a T-shirt. No thermals.

After practice, it took a half-hour for my hands to thaw out enough to grip a pen to autograph a football. At the end of a season it's customary for all the players to sign on a ball for each player to save as a momento.

Bill Parcells didn't yell and scream at us in practice. He didn't have to. We knew what we had to do. We had to beat the Pittsburgh Steelers in order to host San Francisco the following week in the NFC wild-card playoff game. If we lost and Washington and San Francisco won, we would be out of the playoffs. The Steelers won four Super Bowls between 1974 and 1979, but they have been struggling ever since. They came into our game 7–8 and were trying to avoid their first losing season since 1971. "We're not dominating teams like the Steelers used to do in the late seventies," said Pittsburgh defensive back Dwayne Woodruff.

One of my closest friends, six-time Pro-Bowler Donnie Shell, was completing his twelfth season with the Steelers. He came out of South Carolina State two years before me and lives near me in Columbia, S.C.

in the off-season. Some people think about retiring at his age, but Donnie still has that competitive fire. I heard he had addressed his team before their game against Buffalo the previous week. Pittsburgh came from a 21–0 deficit to win 30–24.

I remember when Donnie walked into his first Steelers' camp as a free agent and hit so many people on special teams that he made the squad. He became the first and only special teams' captain Pittsburgh has had. After his first season, his first move was to buy a house for his mother in Whitmire, S.C. The second was write a check to South Carolina State to repay the cost of his education. Donnie was from a family of 10 children and realized that without a lot of other people's help, he would not have made it in life. I was looking forward to seeing him on Saturday—we were playing a day early to accommodate national television.

Donnie's nickname is "Neck" because he doesn't have much of one. He was a linebacker at S.C. State. I was a down lineman, but we both had the same assistant coach working with us and went through all the drills together. He always has been an inspiration to me because he's such a tough son of a bitch. He hits as hard as a linebacker and he's dedicated.

We had not played the Steelers in the regular season since my rookie year, 1976, when they beat us, 27–0. But their offense hadn't changed much. Instead of Franco Harris and Rocky Bleier in the backfield, they had Frank Pollard (901 yards) and Walter Abercrombie (832). John Stallworth, 33, who has four Super Bowl rings, was still going strong. He had made the transition from deep threat to a possession receiver (71 catches, 881 yards). Their game-breaker was Louis Lipps (58 catches, 1,117 yards, 12 TDs). But the thing Pittsburgh lacked was a quarterback. There was no Terry Bradshaw. David Woodley (shoulder) and Mark Malone (concussion) were injured, so Scott Campbell, with one NFL start under his belt, was starting at quarterback. We weren't cocky, though. Look what Schroeder and Pelluer did against us.

Our locker room was closed to the press the day after the Dallas game as we filled out our Pro Bowl ballots. I always take this seriously and I hope my peers do, too. Our receivers' coach, Pat Hodgson, had complete lists of all the starters in the league and flashed them on a projector screen so we could make our choices. He also had complete stats on everybody in the league. I voted only for one Cowboy, Randy White. I didn't think any other Dallas players deserved it.

You can't vote for yourself or teammates. I voted for receivers Mike Quick and James Lofton, tight end Jimmie Giles and running backs Walter Payton and James Wilder. At inside linebacker, I voted for Mike Singletary of Chicago and Carl Ekern of the Rams.

The next day, I got the word that I'd been named to my seventh Pro Bowl in 10 years. Only Singletary got more votes at inside linebacker. Four of my teammates would be going to Hawaii with me: Lawrence Taylor, Leonard Marshall, Phil Simms, and Joe Morris. We represented the most all-stars our team has had since 1963. Simms and Morris were our first offensive players to make it in 13 years! Marshall would wind up the season with a conference-high $15\frac{1}{2}$ sacks, and he edged the Bears' Dan Hampton for NFC defensive lineman of the year.

"This is a great reflection on the New York Giants," our offensive guard Chris Godfrey said. "We're a better-balanced team than we have been in a long time, and we're a better-balanced offense than we have been in a long time."

"I'm in awe," Morris said. "You've got to understand that my only goal before the season was to be better than last year. It's not something I ever planned on doing. It's such an honor. . . . In college, I was honorable mention."

"It's very, very gratifying," Simms said. "It's an understatement to say I'm happy about it. I don't think it makes up for anything or makes me forget [the Dallas loss], but there have been many times in my career when I wondered if I'd ever get a chance to show what I could do. I'm just very happy."

Taylor said, "I'm not talking today. . . . Just another day. . . . Just another thing." It was his fifth Pro Bowl selection in five years. Lawrence was leading us with 100 tackles. I had 94. So I expected to lose out on the $5,000. But I figured I had a good season, considering I come out on passing downs and Lawrence doesn't. I didn't get any interceptions. I didn't have any all-world games. But I played consistently. The Pro Bowl would provide a little extra cash. The winners get $10,000 and the losers $5,000. But we weren't thinking about that in December.

There was no way to wipe away the Dallas loss. We just had to focus on Pittsburgh. Jerome Sally told a reporter, "I'll probably be 77 years old and ready to go to my grave and I won't have forgotten that game. I personally was crushed." But we had incentive. If we didn't win, we were going home. "Now we can't go in the front door," Casey Merrill said. "We've got to go in the utility door, or down the chimney."

The night before the Steelers' game, I got a call at my hotel at 1:30 in the morning to move my car off the street or it would be towed. They had to plow the street because it was snowing. Instead of moving it, I packed up my stuff and drove home. I got a better night's sleep there than I would have at the hotel. I drove back in the morning.

I had cereal for my pregame meal. I never eat heavily on game day. Usually I just have bacon and eggs. Or if it's a preseason game on a Saturday night, I might have fried chicken in the afternoon. I made some calls to friends. I knew our game was going to be nationally televised and I told them we were going to win. I told some of my friends and family in South Carolina to make sure to watch.

Before the game, recalling the rigors of training camp, I wrote this on a blackboard in our locker room:

> *This is what it comes down*
> *to Remember the two-a-days, the*
> *heat, the sweat & all of*
> *the goose shit we laid in in*
> *July? This is it. Let it all*
> *out now, or there may be no*
> *tomorrow. Let's get it on.*

"I was a little worried we might still be down from the Dallas game," Simms said. "But you could tell in the locker room and the warmups that we were ready. We proved that on the first drive."

We took the opening kickoff and drove 71 yards for a touchdown. On our first eight plays, Morris ran seven times for 53 yards and caught a pass for 15. A penalty cost us 10 yards. Morris scored on a nine-yard burst off left guard. We never had to convert a third-down play during the drive.

We held the Steelers without a first down on their first two series. But on the third, Campbell hit passes to tight end Bennie Cunningham and Stallworth to set up Gary Anderson's 26-yard field goal early in the second period to make the score 7–3.

The next time we had the ball, Morris ran to his right, cut back, ran laterally and down the left sideline for a 65-yard touchdown. He lost his shoe en route, but never broke stride. The guy is just amazing. The shoe came off when he slipped Rick Woods' tackle. He outran Shell at the end.

The next time we had the ball, Rob Carpenter made like Morris, running to his left and cutting back for a 46-yard gain to the Pittsburgh 11. Four plays later, Morris scored from the one behind fullback Maurice Carthon's block. Eric Schubert's kick put us ahead, 21–3. It was the fourth time this year Joe had scored three touchdowns in a game.

The Steelers got the ball and went nowhere. On third down, Andy Headen intercepted a Campbell pass at Pittsburgh's 36. Five plays later, Simms passed to Bobby Johnson down the left sideline for 23 yards and a touchdown. This was our best half since the Houston game. We outgained the Steelers 239 yards to 85. They made only five first downs. We were ahead, 28–3. We did not need any more points.

Pittsburgh got a touchdown the first time it had the ball in the second half. Campbell capped a 70-yard drive by throwing a 34-yard pass to Stallworth, who wrestled the ball away from Perry Williams and scored. You have to hand it to the old pro. Even with nothing at stake and the game out of reach, Stallworth was still competing with all he had. But we let the Steelers have only two more first downs after that, dominating them completely.

"That was the worst ass-kicking we've gotten in a long time," Steelers' coach Chuck Noll said.

"It's a very tough defense," said Campbell, limping to a television interview on a gimpy knee, "no doubt about it. They had a tremendous amount at stake, the playoffs and a lot of money were on the line. We didn't have that."

The New York press had a field day in their Sunday papers. The Giants had more coverage than there had been for President Reagan's summit meeting with Soviet leader Gorbachev at Geneva. And the news commentators got on the bandwagon, too. All of a sudden, all of our disappointments and mistakes were forgotten. The media realized that we were three victories away from appearing in the Super Bowl. Their headlines were jingoistic. The world loves a winner.

Beating Pittsburgh was redemption for us. Washington beat St. Louis on the same day, but Dallas lost to San Francisco the next day, 31–16. That gave the Giants, Cowboys, Redskins and 49ers 10–6 records. By besting us twice, the Cowboys won our division title based on the tiebreaker procedure. We were awarded second place. The system also gave us the right to host the 49ers in our first home playoff game in 23 years.

Joe Morris wound up carrying 36 times for 202 yards in the Steelers' game and set a club record with 1,336 rushing yards on the year. We held Pollard to 90 yards in 16 carries and the rest of Steelers to 124 total yards. There was no way we wanted to back into the playoffs. And now we would not. Pittsburgh linebacker Greg Carr said the Steelers were caught over-pursuing Morris, playing too aggressively to get to the ball. Then Morris would cut back and leave them leaning the wrong way. "That's something he does on his own," Carr said.

"They had a lot of cutback stuff," Shell said. "They tried to get us flowing one way and break it back against the grain."

"He's the kind of back that can break your back at any time," Keith Willis said of Morris. "He's determined not to be denied. He just goes out and gets the yardage. He's going to the Pro Bowl and he deserves it. We tried to tackle him and we just didn't wrap him up. You can't do that with a back like him. You have to wrap him up and make sure his knees touch the turf."

"If Joe can get 200 yards," said Rob Carpenter, "why should anybody else get the ball? Last year, they gave up on Butch, tried Tony Galbreath in there [at halfback], and Joe seemed like the last chance. They had to give him a shot. He got his chance and he has been relentless. He never gave up. This didn't come easy. He worked for it."

Morris had to climb up on a table to be interviewed by a horde of reporters. He thanked our strength coach, Johnny Parker, for a conditioning program that helped him survive the season. Parker likes to say, "Never bet against a small man, because he's had to fight all of his life." That's very true in Joe's case. He had 21 touchdowns for us in 1985, only three short of John Riggins' NFL record. I don't think I'll ever forget the sight of him running down the field with only one shoe on. "It was a trap play," Morris said. "Yeah, my sock was flapping, but. . . . He made it

"We've had some tough times this season," said Simms, who had to throw only 16 passes all day, completing 10, "and we've hurt ourselves. But we're in the playoffs and we're mentally ready. I think our strength is that we're solid overall, on offense and defense. . . . What we have this year that we didn't last year is that our running game is dependable."

To win in the NFL, a team must be able to run late in the season when wind, rain, and snow sometimes make passing tough. Morris did a helluva job. But let's not forget the Suburbanites. Our offensive line stayed healthy the whole year and did a good job, too.

"I think we're more confident going into the playoffs this year than we were last year," Chris Godfrey said. "The games we lost were not a reflection of our ability. Winning today helped reinforce that."

21 Game No. 18
Chicago 21
Giants 0

We'll Be Back

LET'S FACE IT: 1985 was the Year of the Bears.

A few games into the season, these guys were so sure they were going to the Super Bowl that they recorded "The Super Bowl Shuffle," a rap record whose proceeds went to charity. By the week before our National Football Conference semifinal playoff game, it had sold 750,000 copies and an additional 150,000 videos.

Not all the Bears approved of doing the record. "I thought it was pretentious," Chicago defensive end Dan Hampton said. "After the Super Bowl, I might have done it."

Bears' defensive tackle Steve McMichael said, "I don't believe in bragging before the fact.

Here's a sample of the lyrics:

> *(Walter Payton:)*
> *Well, they call me Sweetness and I like to dance*
> *Runnin' the ball is like makin' romance.*
> *We've had the goal since training camp*
> *To give Chicago a Super Bowl champ.*
> *And we're not doin' this because we're greedy*
> *The Bears are doin' it to feed the needy.*
> *We didn't come here to look for trouble.*
> *We just come here to do the Super Bowl Shuffle.*
> © Red Label Records, Inc. 1985

The New York–New Jersey media finally discovered the Giants after our victory over the 49ers. GIGANTIC screamed a *Daily News* headline, adding "49ers routed, we're loaded for Bear."

New York *Newsday* said, "Giants Take Super Step" and under a front-page photo of Joe Morris, said he was moving us "closer to the Super Bowl."

The New York Times blared, "Bring on the Chicago Bears."

The folks at NBC-TV, however, were cheering for the Bears against us, hoping that Chicago would make it to Super Bowl XX on Jan. 26. "They are the stars of the NFL this season," an NBC spokesman said. "They have caught the imagination of the nation. It obviously wouldn't hurt the numbers (ratings) if they make it all the way."

The Bears' biggest media star of the year was William Perry, a 308-pound noseguard nicknamed "The Refrigerator," who got national publicity and endorsement contracts after the Bears used him as a running back and pass-catcher in short-yardage situations near their opponents' goal line. The guy even got on the *David Letterman Show*. I was looking forward to a chance to hit him. There's nothing I'd have liked better than to defrost The Refrigerator. I like challenges.

The Bears drew a first-round bye in the playoffs after winning their NFC Central title and had an extra week to let their wounds heal and get ready for us. The Bears left icy Chicago and practiced at the Atlanta Falcons' complex in Suwanee, Ga. Talk about confident. The Bears were.

"We're three games away from where we wanted to be (champions) when the season started," quarterback Jim McMahon said.

Talking about our offensive line and quarterback Phil Simms, Bears' defensive end Richard Dent said, "I've seen better offensive lines . . . He sits back there (in the pocket). He holds the ball longer than most quarterbacks . . . I like that. I think we should have a pretty good day sacking him."

When somebody asked Dent if he minded that Bears' fans were barred from the team's Georgia practice site, he said, "they'll see us in the Super Bowl."

The Bears were hosting their first playoff game at Soldier Field since 1963, when they beat the Giants 14–10, in the NFL championship game. Their coach, Mike Ditka, was a tight end on that Chicago team. Both teams went into a long decline after that. But in 1985, Chicago put it all together. The Bears had the earliest division title-clinching in the NFL in the eleventh week of the season. Their only loss came to the Miami Dolphins.

Chicago had all sorts of numbers on its side. It led the NFL in total defense (allowing only 258 yards a game) and in interceptions (34). It led the NFC in scoring (456 points) and rushing average (173 yards a game). It was 17–2 in its past 19 home games, 8–0 in 1985. It was 23–4 in McMahon's last 27 starts. But the Bears' offense still revolved around Payton, who had one of the best years in his career with 1,551 yards rushing, 49 catches for 483 yards, and 11 touchdowns.

Payton is the toughest player I ever have played against. Our game marked his 153rd straight start. Most backs are just happy to get through a season in one piece. But this guy has been healthy his entire career and has rushed for an NFL record 14,860 career yards. I've talked to him at Pro Bowls. He's a practical joker, a great guy. He keeps everybody loose, but he doesn't boast or brag. He's very humble. And he's not a flashy dresser. Just one of the guys. I've never told him how much I respect him. Some day I will.

The only regular-season game I ever played against him was the last game in 1977 in the snow and sleet. Payton needed 201 to break O.J.'s season record of 2,003 yards. We didn't want him to get it against us. I got 15 tackles and helped hold him to 47 yards in 15 carries. But we lost, 12–9, in overtime.

For his size, Payton took a lot of abuse in his career and never missed a game or was badly hurt in 11 seasons. He played with his heart, even when he didn't have good blockers in front of him. Our careers are a lot alike. We've both played for a lot of losing teams and we're both finishing up with winners.

The Bears had Walter for a decade and never got to a championship game. The secret to their success in 1985 was their innovative "46" defense, named after former Bear Doug Plank, who wore that number. It was conceived by their defensive coordinator, Buddy Ryan. In it, Bears' linebackers Otis Wilson and Wilber Marshall line up on the line of scrimmage outside of the left end, creating a six-man front. They usually drop off in pass coverage but the offense must respect the possibility of a six-man rush.

The Bears also blitzed an inside linebacker, a safety, or a cornerback at times. The defense was a gambling, aggressive, pressure defense. Because Chicago usually rushed six players on passing downs, opposing offensive lines could not double-team anybody. Their cornerbacks often were in single coverage. so, theoretically, they were vulnerable to big plays. The Dolphins' Dan Marino beat them, 38–24, by taking three-step drops and hitting quick passes.

So our top priority was to devise an offensive game plan to defeat the Bears' 46 defense. Ryan told a reporter, "A week isn't enough for the Giants or any other team to prepare for our defense." As it turned out, he was right, but we were sky-high the week before the game.

On Thursday in the Greenwich Village section of Manhattan, six refrigerators were flattened in front of 72 Perry Street (Perry wore No. 72) by a 16,000-pound van christened "Heavy Metal." The driver, Mike Trinagel, said, "We want to show the Bears what New York is made of, and what the Giants are going to do to The Refrigerator."

A couple of days earlier, a Giants' fan delivered a refrigerator to the front lawn of our left guard Billy Ard. Ard drove to Giants Stadium for practice and when he emerged afterwards, there was the refrigerator at the player's gate.

The funniest thing that happened during the week was when the New Jersey Division of Consumer Affairs issued a press release alleging that our punter, Sean Landeta, had scalped tickets to our San Francisco game the previous week. He was accused of selling $22 and $25 tickets for $50. He supposedly threw in autographed photos of himself. Scalping for more than a 10 per cent profit in New Jersey is illegal.

We players loved it. Lawrence Taylor set up a fake ticket booth in front of Landeta's locker reading, "Tickets and photos for sale here! $50." After practice, linebacker Carl Banks strolled by Landeta's locker and sing-songed, "Anybody got any tickets to sell?" Landeta denied the scalping charges.

We had a lot of concern about our secondary because several of our guys were banged up. Free safety Terry Kinard acknowledged that his left thumb had been broken in the Steelers' game on Dec. 21. He was wearing a cast that ended halfway up his forearm. Others hurt were Elvis Patterson (sprained foot and ankle), Ted Watts (bruised knee), and Kenny Hill (hyperextended knee). But all managed to practice during the week.

"Adrenaline is a remarkably potent endorphin," said Hill, a Yale graduate with a degree in molecular biophysics.

Joe Morris showed his gratitude to the people who made it possible for him to have the season he did by buying watches for 13 offensive teammates. There was a Super Bowl atmosphere in our dressing room during the week, with dozens of reporters and television cameras every day. The stadium security guards made up a sign for our locker room door that said, "Bear season now open." We were brimming with confidence.

"Chicago has really become the darlings of the media this year," Hill said. "They're something of a hybrid. They're mean and vicious like the Raiders and yet they're media favorites like the Cowboys used to be. But I think we're recognized as a very good football team by people who really know football.''

"Everyone should realize by now," Jim Burt said, "we're not like the Giants teams of the past. We've lost six games but we gave away four or five of them and were competitive in every game. We've been in close games. We know how to react to pressure.''

Byron Williams said, "We haven't had our butts kicked in any game.''

There's a first time for everything.

Game day dawned sunny and stayed that way. I had a lot of pregame anxiety. I was thinking to myself that if I felt so nervous before this game, how would I feel before a Super Bowl? At the pregame meal, I looked around and saw some guys who were so nervous they couldn't eat. They looked like if they did eat, they would throw up.

I went out before the warmups in only a T-shirt, although the temperature was 14 degrees, the wind was 15 mph from the west and the wind-chill factor made it feel like −13. I volunteered to help the ground crew roll the tarpaulin off the field. They were kidding me about the weather. I said, "hey, guys, it's not cold.'' They were telling me, "We're going to beat you.'' I asked one of them, "What number do *you* wear?''

During the introductions, I was checking out the Honey Bears cheerleaders. It was so cold that I was wearing skin-diver's rubber gloves. But I did not think the weather was a real factor in the game, except for the wind, which made a few passes by both quarterbacks flutter.

I called heads and won the coin toss. In our first series, a 14-yard run by Joe Morris gave us a first down at our 40 yard-line. But on second-and-10 our fullback, Rob Carpenter caught a pass over the middle, was hit by Wilber Marshall, and fumbled. The Bears' linebacker Mike Singletary recovered at their 49. Carpenter had not fumbled in his preceding 22 games.

No problem. Our defense held the Bears—three downs and punt —twice in a row. Our offense went nowhere, either. Simms was sacked by Dent to set up a fourth-and-20 at our 12. Then came a play I'll never forget as long as I live.

Landeta moved forward to punt the ball. As he dropped it toward his foot, a gust of wind blew it to the right. He followed through and only brushed the side of the ball, which dropped straight down. The Bears' Shaun Gayle picked it up seven yards behind the line of scrimmage and ran five yards for a touchdown. Kevin Butler's PAT put Chicago ahead, 7–0 at 9:32.

"A freak accident," Landeta said later. "You know the wind moves the ball, but you figure you'll get at least a piece of it, even if it goes only 20 yards. Of all the thousands and thousands and thousands of punts I've had in practice and games, that's never, ever happened. It's just unfortunate it had to happen in a game like this and cost us a touchdown."

"I was five yards down the field before I realized he never even got to hit the ball," our center Bart Oates said.

"Coach Parcells had a look of disbelief on his face," Landeta said. "He couldn't understand it. I told him I couldn't understand it, either . . . Even if you try to miss a punt after you've thrown the ball in the air, it'd be almost impossible."

I told everybody to forget it and try to concentrate on their jobs. It was still early in the game. We came back from adversity several times during the year. But we all could not help wondering why these weird things have to happen to us.

In the rest of the first half, the Bears moved the ball better than we did, but neither team got any points. Butler missed field goal tries of 26 and 49 yards. Eric Schubert's 19-yarder for us with 11 seconds left in the half hit the left upright. It was amazing how many problems our kickers caused us in the 1985 season. By the end of the year, we had no faith in either of them. Two years previously the kickers were two of our best players.

Not getting anything at the end of the half really hurt. Simms had completed passes of 31 yards to George Adams and 17 yards to Bobby Johnson to bring up a first-and-goal at the Bears' two with 29 seconds left and no time outs. "If we ran the ball and got into a pile," Simms said, "the clock could have run out on us. So we threw."

He threw three straight incompletions under pressure and we had to try the field goal. On the first incompletion, the ball fluttered in the wind, brushed Johnson's helmet, and went between his gloves.

"It was the same play as the one I had just caught," Johnson said. "I should have caught that one."

And Schubert should have made the field goal. I was lined up on the left wing and, after I blocked my man, I saw the ball hit off the post. It didn't bother me, though. I still thought we could come back.

"I hit it perfect," Schubert said. "I thought it was right down the middle. Then the damn goalpost jumped up and blocked it." Schubert, the midseason media darling, missed six of his last seven and might have kicked his way off the team.

"I lined up wrong," he said. "I was on the hash mark and I kicked it right down the hash into the upright."

"When they couldn't score on the last possession of the half," the Bears' Otis Wilson said, "that told us that we could hold them."

"It was the most important part of the game," Bears' safety Gary Fencik said.

"After what happened in the first half," Casey Merrill said, "I thought this just wasn't God's will that we win."

Our defense limited the Bears to 145 yards in the first half, so we felt we had done well. But our offense got only 78 yards—a season low. We were down 7-0, but we felt we had played the best team in pro football pretty tough.

Butler missed another field goal, from 38 yards, early in the third quarter. Then our offense went three downs and out three times in a row. Simms "generated" minus-12, plus-three, minus-five, and plus-three yards in the first four series in the second half. Our defense was on the field too long. We got tired and eventually broke under the pressure.

"It was a match of two great defenses," our offensive right tackle Karl Nelson said. "We just left ours out on the field too long." It's been that way often in my career.

A Singletary sack of Simms pushed our offense back to our nine. Then Landeta got off a miserable 32-yard punt. So the Bears took over at our 41. Three Matt Suhey runs gained 18 yards before McMahon's 23-yard touchdown pass to Dennis McKinnon, who wrestled the ball away from Patterson in the right corner of the end zone. The ball nicked Patterson's helmet on the way down. Linebackers Andy Headen and Lawrence Taylor were blitzing on the play. Butler's PAT made the score 14–0.

"We had three guys in the area," McMahon said of the TD pass, "so I just threw it there and Dennis caught it."

"He ran a 'go,'" Patterson said. "I turned, the ball was there, and then all of a sudden it disappeared. I don't know where it went."

"It's the Windy City, right?" Perry Williams said.

The Bears' receivers did a better job than our guys did at adjusting to windblown balls, probably because they are used to their home conditions. None of the passes were pinpoint passes. The wind played tricks with them. It was up to our secondary to go up and wrestle the ball away from the Bear receivers. They didn't do it.

Late in the third period, McMahon hit tight end Tim Wrightman for 46 yards to our 20. McMahon beat a blitz by Taylor and Williams on the play. "It was a breakdown in our coverage," Gary Reasons said. "They quick-counted us and we left the tight end uncovered over the middle."

Then McMahon hit McKinnon on a 20-yard touchdown pass to ice the game. "The Giants were in a blitz situation," McMahon said, "so I called an audible for a down-and-in to Dennis and he just beat his man."

It was Elvis again. "McMahon made a great throw," Patterson said, "and McKinnon a great catch. He hit a seam. It's one of those things. I saw the ball all the way on that one."

Taylor blitzed on that play, too, but he didn't get McMahon.

Simms passed us down the field into Bears' territory twice in the last period but both drives ended on fourth-down failures at Chicago's 27 and 29.

"By the end of the third quarter," the Bears' Hampton said, "you could see it in their eyes. They were ready to get on a bus and go home. Simms didn't have a clue about what we were doing."

"I think it would be fair to say," our guard Chris Godfrey said, "that Chicago deserved to win this game."

Simms, bothered by the flu, wound up being sacked six times, hurried five times, and knocked down nine times. He completed only 14 of 35 passes for 209 yards. We got only 32 yards rushing. So it was complete domination by the Bears. Their offense didn't show me a lot, but they outgained us 363 yards to 181. We were 0-for-14 on third- and fourth-down conversions.

"They beat us physically," Simms said. "Sick or not, I wouldn't have played any better. Our stadium is windy, too. That's no excuse. I threw most of the passes, except for one or two, where I wanted to. I just didn't have all day to make a decision, and we weren't getting open as well as we thought. Several times I had to just throw it away."

"The thing that bothered me most," Godfrey said, "was losing the fumble (by Carpenter) on the first drive. . . . We seemed to be in control, doing what we needed to do."

My overall impression was that we did not play with the same intensity as a team that we had the previous week. Our defense did its best, but the Bears' defense shut down our offense completely. They deserve credit for that.

"They're tendency-oriented," the Bears' Dent said of our offense. "In each formation they use, they have certain tendencies that we predicted in our game plan. And they didn't let us down."

I think what Dent said is true. I'm sure our offensive coordinator Ron Erhardt will be working hard to vary our offense. I'm no offensive expert, but I do know we have to be able to run more plays out of the same formations and be less predictable. Still, the Bears' defense has a remarkable collection of athletes. They made a lot of teams look bad last season.

"They totally took us out of any flow we tried to get into," our center Oates said. "I was surprised, very surprised. We'd come off the field, series after series, and say to ourselves, 'What have we got to do to make this thing work?'"

Our defensive coordinator Bill Belichick put in some second-half blitzes because we had to gamble when we were behind. But McMahon beat most of them. "Sometimes it works," Belichick said. "This time we paid for it. But we shut them out in the first half and we were still down, 7–0."

"Their line was good," Merrill said of the Bears. "They were cocky. They're 16–1. They have a right to be. They walked with their chins up, chests out, arms back." Like Marines.

"What will I remember about 1985?" Merrill was asked. "The great feeling of beating San Francisco last week . . . (and) the empty feeling of Soldier Field, where 400 people in blue jerseys were chasing Phil Simms."

I'm going to remember Landeta's nonpunt. So is Sean. "Anytime a crazy play like that happens," Landeta said, "people are going to remember. Especially when it happens in a playoff game."

"That's football," said Oates.

"It was a good year up until now," Godfrey said. "This kind of spoils everything. But we (linemen) agreed that the Bears are a lot quicker overall than we thought they were."

 **Postmortem**

OUR CO-OWNER Wellington Mara told reporters that we were competitive in 22 games this year (16–6 including exhibitions and the 49er playoff game) before losing to Chicago. "Go back to last year," Mara said. "The Bears lost to the 49ers, 23–0, for the NFC title. If they can improve that much, we can, too. You're certainly not satisfied unless you're number one. But let's face it. Only four teams went further than we did. And a lot of our young players haven't reached their potential."

"The Giants [of 1986] can be the Bears of 1985," Reasons said. "We're talking about it already. We've got a lot of quality players here, a winning attitude. I think it's going to carry over."

"If I was a betting man," Merrill said, "I'd say this is going to be a winning franchise for a couple of years."

I don't know how many wait-'til-next-years I can take. A player can play as long as he wants, if he has the enthusiasm and desire. Look at Pete Rose. He's 45 and still playing major-league baseball. I still feel the same excitement now when I take the field as I did when I was a rookie. But the older you get, the more you think about retiring. But I think the Giants are committed to winning. Especially coach Parcells.

"I'm not looking to do my job just well enough to keep it," he told reporters the day after our season ended. "I don't think it's possible in New York to keep expectations down. You don't get any satisfaction out of winning wild-card games. I just want to get into a championship game and I'm not going to rest 'til I get there.

"On the other hand," he said, "we were fortunate in that we had a lot of guys come in and do a good job for us right away. Mark Bavaro, Bart Oates. . . . If there's any sense of satisfaction, it comes from the competitiveness of the team. We have players on this team who figure they're going to find a way to win. All season, I never felt, 'Oh, damn, we're not going to win this one.'"

Meanwhile, our players were cleaning out their lockers and scattering. Parcells was making plans to go to the Super Bowl in New Orleans on January 26 and stay there for the scouting combine workouts of college players. George Young was planning to attend college all-star games to rate prospects. Phil McConkey said he was going to inquire about a job in sports broadcasting. Merrill was leaving for his desert home in Borrego Springs, California. Burt was preparing to open a Seven-11 store in Midland Park, N.J. and buying another one in Buffalo. Backup quarterback Jeff Rutledge asked Parcells for a trade before heading back to his home on the West Coast. Mark Haynes knew he was cleaning out his locker for the last time.

Pro football isn't a Utopia or a fairytale land. The Giants are like a family, and families have differences. Some players have personality clashes and they wind up leaving. Others have personal problems. Like Taylor.

I don't think Lawrence's drug problem is going to derail his career. He realized he had a problem and took care of it. I respect that. Nobody busted him. He wasn't caught dealing. I think with a little willpower and support from the rest of us, he can come back and be an all-pro in 1986.

It's amazing how you think you know somebody and you don't really know them. I took the Giants' Pro Bowl contingent out to dinner this past February in Honolulu at a place called Nick's Fish Market. I left on Super Bowl Sunday. I knew the Bears would beat New England. I just didn't think it would be that bad (46–10). I was airborne while the game was in progress. I don't intend to watch the film.

Anyway, everything seemed fine with Lawrence in Hawaii. He had brought his wife, his two children, his housekeeper, and a friend, Paul Davis. Lawrence wound up leaving some jewelry in his hotel room after he checked out. The hotel staff gave it to me. When I came back from the Pro Bowl, I drove to Lawrence's house in Upper Saddle River, N.J. Davis answered the door, took the jewelry, thanked me, and said Lawrence had gone away for a while. He didn't say where. A few days later, Howard Cosell broke L.T.'s story.

*   *   *

Management was considering shifting George Adams to fullback next to Morris and using Maurice Carthon to back up Adams. As this book goes to press, Morris has ended a 22-day holdout in time to play our last preseason game. But he has not signed a new contract and is unhappy.

Meanwhile, other familiar faces have disappeared. Tight end Don Hasselback's contract was not renewed. Casey Merrill was traded to Cleveland. Others released before the regular season began were kicker Eric Shubert, cornerback Ted Watts, offensive tackles Gordon King and Conrad Goode, defensive end Dee Hardison, and receivers Phil Mc-Conkey and Byron Williams. These players were placed on the IR list: running back George Adams, guard David Jordan, defensive Curtis McGriff, and kicker Ali Haji-Sheikh (Bob Thomas was signed to replace him.)

So my reflections about the roster on the plane coming home from Chicago had come true. For opening day against Dallas we lined up without 13 players who were on the squad for the Bears playoff game. Change is part of the NFL. If you don't improve each year, you lose. Despite the changes, my task is the same as always: winning the battle at the point of attack.